THE FOUNTAINWELL DRAMA TEXTS

General Editors

ARTHUR BROWN

T. A. DUNN

ANDREW GURR

JOHN HORDEN

A. NORMAN JEFFARES

BRIAN W. M. SCOBIE

JEREMY V. STEELE

17

WILLIAM CONGREVE

THE WAY OF THE WORLD

Edited by
JOHN BARNARD

Audire est Operæ pretium, procedere recte
Qui mæchis non vultis—   Hor. Sat. 2 .1. 1.
—Metuat doti deprensa.—   Ibid.

OLIVER AND BOYD
EDINBURGH
1972

OLIVER AND BOYD
Tweeddale Court
14 High Street
Edinburgh EH1 1YL

A Division of Longman Group Ltd

First Published 1972

Hardback 0 05 002452 3
Paperback 0 05 002451 5

Printed in Great Britain by
Cox & Wyman Ltd
London, Fakenham and Reading

ACKNOWLEDGMENTS

This edition of *The Way of the World* owes a considerable and obvious debt to the work of other scholars, especially to the editorial work of the late Professor H. J. Davis, and that of F. W. Bateson and Professor A. Norman Jeffares. For constant encouragement and wise advice when first starting work on Congreve's comedies, I am deeply grateful to the patient and humane scholarship of Professor Davis and F. W. Bateson.

The shrewdness and generosity of the Textual General Editor of this volume, Professor A. J. Gurr, have enabled me to avoid several errors and deficiencies, and B. W. M. Scobie's painstaking help was invaluable in preparing the edition for the press.

Leeds   JOHN BARNARD
December 1968

CONTENTS

CRITICAL INTRODUCTION

The Way of the World hides behind its own brilliance. Its tightly worked surface, its artificiality, the complicated plot and *dénouement*, all hold off the audience. Even the characters are distanced from their own emotions—Mirabell's analysis of his mistress is more dispassionate than that of the worldly-wise Fainall:

> FAINALL.   You do her wrong; for to give her her Due, she has Wit.
>
> MIRABELL.   She has Beauty enough to make any Man think so; and Complaisance enough not to contradict him who shall tell her so.[1]

Judgment, analysis, antithesis—these qualities dominate in a comedy concerned with the necessary decorum and artifices through which individual feeling must fulfil itself within a society where love easily founders on cold financial calculation. An audience which admires Albee's stripping down to the psychological buff, or Beckett's blank anatomy of the human condition, may find *The Way of the World* a difficult comedy to appreciate.

Twentieth-century preconceptions can hinder a clear view of *The Way of the World*. Until recently, criticism of Restoration comedy has done little to help. Charles Lamb, embarrassed by the promiscuity and obscenity of its heroes, attempted to rescue the "artificial comedy of the last age" by evacuating it to an aesthetic enclave reserved for "high camp" frivolities.[2] This defensive strategy, adopted by later critics, is as prejudicial to *The Way of the World* as the puritanical rigour with which L. C. Knights, in an influential essay, wrote that the

---

[1] *The Way of the World* (this edition, hereafter cited as *W.W.*) I. I. 134–8.

[2] "On the Artificial Comedy of the Last Century," in *Essays of Elia* (1823). For similar arguments, see William Hazlitt, *Lectures on the English Comic Writers* (1819), J. L. Palmer, *The Comedy of Manners* (1913), and T. H. Fujimura, *The Restoration Comedy of Wit* (1952), p. 62. For these and other books listed in the Bibliography (pp. 114–17) full publishing details have not been given in footnotes.

difficulty ". . . is not that the comedies are 'immoral', but that they are trivial, gross, and dull".[3]

The most long-standing criticism of *The Way of the World* itself is that it suffers from having many "witty things" but "no plot".[4] Critics like Bonamy Dobrée and Allardyce Nicoll happily throw away the plot in exchange for the brilliance of the proviso scene—"the *dénouement* is forced, a mere trumped up affair, but it does not matter."[5] Acknowledged by them as a masterpiece, *The Way of the World* lacked themes or pattern, and had a plot which was minimal at best, and incomprehensible at worst. More demanding critics might well echo Harley Granville-Barker's query of Restoration comedy in general—"How could an audience both be clever enough to understand the story and stupid enough to be interested by it when they did ?"[6]

In fact, the structure of *The Way of the World* is central to its effectiveness, and Congreve's brilliant surface is neither heartless nor self-regarding—unless it is seen through the distorting mirror of *The Importance of Being Ernest*. *The Way of the World* is not about the stylised pirouettes of a "gay couple". Congreve's concerns and themes spring from the difficulties which confront the individual's need to fulfil his inner self and yet attain material security (pay his mortgage and keep his soul), and to reconcile sexual gratification with respect for his partner's integrity as a human being. These problems are the more pointed for being posed in a society which lacked the protections of the Married Women's Property Acts, and in which the financial security of both young men and young women was dependent on the whims of an elder generation. Like a great deal of Restoration comedy, *The Way of the World* attacks the customary *mariage de convenance* in the late seventeenth-century upper and middle classes,

[3] "Restoration Comedy: The Reality and the Myth", in *Scrutiny*, VI (1937), p. 140. Reprinted in *Explorations*. See also, John Wain, "Restoration Comedy and its Modern Critics" in *Preliminary Essays* (1957).

[4] Quotation from Lady Marow, a member of the early audience, Dartmouth Mss., vol. III, *HMC*, 15th Report, Appendix Part I, p. 145. London 1896.

[5] B. Dobrée, *Restoration Comedy: 1660–1720* (1924), p. 148. For Nicoll's view, see *History of the English Drama: 1660–1900*, vol. I, *Restoration Drama: 1660–1700* (4th ed., 1952), p. 243.

[6] H. Granville-Barker, *On Dramatic Method*, p. 117. London (Sidgwick & Jackson), 1931.

and argues that love is not about money or "interest", but about feeling.[7]

Congreve's themes are built into the structure of the play.[8] The comedy, as Paul and Miriam Mueschke first pointed out,[9] is a legacy conflict. Two sets of people—the pair of adulterers, Fainall and Mrs Marwood, as against Mirabell, Millamant and Mrs Fainall—struggle to gain control of the superannuated coquette, Lady Wishfort, in whose power lies the fortune of her daughter, Mrs Fainall, and half the fortune of her niece, Millamant. All the contrivances and subterfuges are directed to this single end. If the convolutions of *The Way of the World* result from the complicated legal and family relationships,[10] they also result from the characters' past actions. The Mueschkes have noted that "every character who has indulged in illicit relations finds that his present or past adultery hampers his ability to plan for the future—that immorality cannot be quibbled out of existence."[11] All the main characters have something to hide from one another and from Lady Wishfort: dissimulation is crucial.

The main characters' dependence upon Lady Wishfort's irrevocable disposition of the legacies is absolute. Inherited property, and that only, provides both wealth and income. If their privileged middle-class ethos seems narrowly unrepresentative, it is worth remembering that contemporary Puritan attitudes were, if anything, more mercenary—and prudish into the bargain.[12]

The plot depends upon the fact that Millamant loses half her fortune if she marries without Lady Wishfort's consent. Mirabell's problem is to gain her in marriage without losing that half. Unfortunately, he is *persona non grata* with Lady Wishfort, to whom he pretended love in order to gain access to his mistress. He has also compromised Mrs

---

[7] See P. F. Vernon, "Marriage of Convenience and the Moral Code of Restoration Comedy", in *Essays in Criticism*, XII (1962), pp. 370–87.

[8] His Dedication (ll. 53–6) demands that a discriminating audience appreciate "the artful Solution of the *Fable*" unlike the "Multitude . . . who come with expectation to Laugh out the last Act of a Play. . . ."

[9] Paul and Miriam Mueschke, *A New View of Congreve's Way of the World* (1958).

[10] For a family tree of the Wishfort family, see Appendix (p. 127).

[11] P. and M. Mueschke, *op. cit.*, p. 14.

[12] See Christopher Hill's extremely suggestive essay, "Clarissa Harlowe and her Times", in *Essays in Criticism*, V (1955), pp. 315–40. Reprinted in *Puritanism and Revolution*. London (Secker & Warburg), 1958.

Fainall while she was still a widow, and arranged her marriage with Fainall when they feared she was pregnant. Fainall married for money to support his liaison with the passionate Mrs Marwood (who secretly desires Mirabell). Fainall and Mrs Marwood attempt to blackmail Lady Wishfort with the threat of exposing her daughter's affair with Mirabell, hoping thereby to force Lady Wishfort to surrender Mrs Fainall's fortune to them, as well as the half of Millamant's fortune which she forfeits when she refuses her aunt's choice, Sir Wilfull Witwoud. In reply, the Mirabell faction, which increases in size as the play develops, attempts various delaying tactics, although the ultimate defeat of Fainall and Mrs Marwood is due not to dissimulation, but to a deed of trust, which appoints Mirabell trustee of Mrs Fainall's fortune.

Congreve patterns his action round opposed pairs. The two illicit affairs between Mirabell and Mrs Fainall, and Fainall and Mrs Marwood, contrast "the progressive regeneration of one pair of adulterers ... with the progressive degeneration of another pair of adulterers."[13] This antithetical pairing appears everywhere in the comedy. Fainall's marriage, based on mere "interest", is set against the prospective marriage of Mirabell and Millamant, which is based on trust and mutual respect. The two wits, Fainall and Mirabell, are the norms by which Witwoud and Petulant must be measured. Further, individuals are set one against the other. Just as the two would-be wits differ sharply, so the first act distinguishes carefully between the somewhat "sententious" Mirabell, concerned for others' feelings, and the "experienced" Fainall. In addition, the younger generation is opposed to its parents' generation, represented in this play only by Lady Wishfort and, to some extent, Sir Wilfull—who further serves to contrast town and country.

These pairs and paired couples allow *The Way of the World* to explore its ethical problems dialectically. The differing "ways of the world" endorsed by Mirabell and Fainall question one another. Fainall regards his own adultery and his wife's indiscretion with Mirabell as but the "Way of the *World*" (III. I. 571–2), and the logical outcome of his attitude is the use of that knowledge for personal gain. But Fainall's success is short-lived: the cynical adulterer has calculated neither on

[13] P. and M. Mueschke, *op. cit.*, p. 9. For the dialectical nature of the play, see Norman N. Holland's perceptive discussion in his *The First Modern Comedies* (1959). My account of the comedy is considerably indebted to both of these books.

the excesses of Mrs Marwood's passion, nor on the possibilities of "generosity" (a key word in the play).[14] He is therefore wholly unprepared for Mirabell's forethought in having Mrs Fainall put her fortune in his trust, a precaution which Mirabell describes as "*the way of the World*, Sir: of the Widdows of the World" (v. 1. 504–5). That is, deception and adultery must be acknowledged to exist in the world, and the only feasible way to live satisfactorily is by observing the rights of individuals and by using the law to protect their rights. Mirabell thereby regenerates himself from rakishness, and simultaneously creates a network of gratitude and trust. Where Mirabell builds up a new society to replace Lady Wishfort's moribund generation, Fainall and Mrs Marwood are progressively isolated. By the end even the fools, through their drunken signatures, are supporters of Mirabell. Fainall must be rejected because his Hobbesian search for power, and his libertine drive to satisfy his appetite, destroy the foundations of any possible society.

The Way of the World considers the bases of a viable complementary relationship in marriage. Hence the motto on the title-page, taken from Horace's *Satires*, points to what happens when mutual feelings are replaced by adultery and "interest",[15] while the conclusion gives an admonition, significantly cast in a legal metaphor—that of fraud:

> From hence let those be warn'd, who mean to wed;
> Lest mutual falsehood stain the Bridal-Bed:
> For each deceiver to his cost may find,
> That marriage frauds too oft are paid in kind.[16]

The neatness with which *The Way of the World* may be schematised raises the question of how critics managed to miss its firm structure. In part the answer lies in Congreve's adoption of the "rules" formulated by neoclassical theorists for a "regular" drama. There are

[14] Clifford Leech gives an illuminating account of *The Way of the World*'s place in the developing sentimentality of the 1690s in "Congreve and the Century's End", in *Philological Quarterly*, XLI (1962), pp. 275–93. The place of "generosity" in this context is obvious, but there are important differences between it and "sentimentality".

[15] "It is worth your while to listen, you who don't want things to turn out well for adulterers . . . she who is found out fears for her dowry" (Horace, *Satires*, I. II. 37–8, 131).

[16] *W.W.*, v. 1. 564–7.

discreet pointers to Congreve's intentions in this matter.[17] "Regularity" meant obedience to the three unities, observance of the *liaison des scènes*, and the proper use of "intervals" and "hints".[18] This is undoubtedly a partial cause of the characteristic economy of Congreve's play, which sets him apart from other important comic dramatists of the Restoration who had no compunction about ignoring the "rules". In particular, Congreve's use of the "Interval" between the fourth and fifth acts to throw off the "*superfluitez*" of his plot, allows a swift move towards the *dénouement*—but unless the audience listens carefully to the events recounted in the opening exchanges, it is virtually impossible to catch up with the action. Similarly, the crucial "black box" containing the deed of trust seems like a *deus ex machina* unless the "hints" dropped earlier in the play have been picked up.[19]

These devices would be mere pedantry, if it were not that the glancing allusions put the audience into the same relationship *vis-à-vis* the comedy, as that which the characters have with the events in the play. The audience, like the dramatis personae, must, on the basis of barely sufficient evidence, tell appearances from reality.

Moreover, the verisimilitude of "regularity" forced Congreve to construct a rigidly logical plot. The strict causality of plot demanded becomes both a condition and an expression of *The Way of the World*'s universe. Wit can no longer gloss over the fact of adultery, though judgment and generosity may mitigate its effect. Yet since this verisimilitude is itself an "artful" imitation of reality, *The Way of the World* partakes in a very particular way of that "combined plausibility and separateness" which Clifford Leech has noted as typical of the Restoration stage.[20] The finish and artifice of *The Way of the World*'s regular structure contrasts with the strong feelings it constrains, just as

[17] See Note on Text (pp. 10–14). Further evidence of Congreve's abiding interest in "regularity" can be found in *The Double-Dealer* and its preface, in the essay on the Pindaric ode, and in the critical works in his library. For the latter, see *The Library of William Congreve*, ed. J. C. Hodges (1955). See also Commentary, Dedication, l. 52.

[18] For a full, and exhaustively pedantic, account of these devices, see F. Hèdelin, Abbé d'Aubignac, *La practique du theatre*, pp. 163–73, 309. Paris, 1669. Congreve owned both a French edition and the English translation.

[19] For an outline of the clues dropped in the course of the play, see P. and M. Mueschke, *op. cit.*, p. 13. They do not, however, make the connection with the use of "hints".

[20] Leech, "Congreve and the Century's End", pp. 285–6. See also Holland, *The First Modern Comedies*, pp. 236–7.

the antithetical and epigrammatic dialogue shields the deeper emotions of its characters.

Regularity thereby carries over to the articulation and form of *The Way of the World* the decorums and propriety which govern its conversation. The conflict between Fainall and Mirabell is, from one aspect, one about the function of manners and social propriety. Fainall clearly considers these as merely another useful division between appearance and reality, to be utilised for his own ends by anyone intelligent enough. For Mirabell the proprieties are a social code controlling the passions, and allowing the individual to preserve his identity. Millamant and Mrs Marwood show the same divergence. The latter's social competence enables her to manipulate Lady Wishfort, while disguising the chaos of her own wildly passionate nature. Millamant's affectation is altogether different. It allows her to head off Mrs Marwood's jealousy (III. I. 255ff.), and, in her relationship with Mirabell, it allows her freedom to explore the nature and depth of feeling which exists between herself and her lover. Both social and artistic decorum in *The Way of the World* restrain the excesses of unfettered nature while retaining the benefits of naturalness. Congreve's attention to the dramatic rules creates a structure which, in its sobriety and restraint, is a perfect analogue for the society created by Mirabell.

At another level, the correspondence between regular structure and thematic pattern appears in the insistence upon law and legality.[21] Law restrains and orders man in society, yet those laws are man-made. *The Way of the World* sees marriage settlements and trusts as, at their best, a contractual expression and embodiment of personal relationships. The legal itemising of the proviso scene (IV. I. 195 ff.) is a metaphor central to the play. Both Millamant and Mirabell must maintain their individual rights, but respect their partner's. To an important extent, Mirabell must regard his future wife as a property—they are, after all, investing their lives in one another. Equally, Millamant's affectation has to do, not with coyness, but with the fact that she must be sure of herself and of Mirabell, "If *Mirabell* shou'd not make a good Husband, I am a lost thing;—for I find I love him violently" (IV. I.

---

[21] The incidence of words carrying legal connotations or overtones enforces this insistence (see Glossary). J. C. Hodges points out that Congreve's legal training at the Middle Temple is evident in this play and in *Love for Love*. See Hodges, *William Congreve the Man* (1941), p. 192.

292–3). Indeed—for her rights within marriage will depend wholly upon Mirabell. Consequently, it is the law and not the intrigue of a wit which resolves the comedy. Sir Wilfull's "instrument", his sword, is pitifully unable to hack Fainall's "Instrument of *Ram Vellam to shreds*" (v. i. 385–6), and Fainall can only be defeated by "*A deed of Conveyance of the whole Estate real of* Arabella Languish *Widdow in Trust to* Edward Mirabell".[22] Mirabell's forethought is endorsed by the law and by society, for Mrs Fainall made out the deed of trust only at "the wholesome advice of Friends and of Sages learned in the Laws of this Land. . . ." (v. i. 495–502).

Over-emphasis on the structure and themes of the comedy at the expense of its wit and humour distorts *The Way of the World*, and a brief account of the play cannot do justice to Congreve's achievement. On the other hand, the vitality of language and characterisation is self-evident. *The Way of the World*, one of the greatest Restoration comedies, is a mature and humane exploration of the necessary artifices of feeling and passion. It rejects dissimulation in favour of lasting and reciprocal relations between man and woman.

The Way of the World was first acted on or about 5 March 1700 at a crucial point in the fortunes of Thomas Betterton's Lincoln's Inn Fields theatre. Since 1695, when Betterton seceded from the established Theatre Royal company, Congreve had been a shareholder in Betterton's group as well as a contracted playwright.[23] At the end of 1699 the company was endangered by the success of its rivals at Drury Lane, where their new playwright, George Farquhar, was enjoying a sensational run with his *Constant Couple*. On Christmas Day 1699, Sir John Vanbrugh wrote, "Matters are running very low with [Betterton's company] this winter: if Congreve's play don't help 'em they are undone."[24]

The Way of the World was not quite the resounding success Better-

---

[22] Congreve's legal resolution of complex human problems was not, in all probability, restricted to his art. He seems to have made a complicated arrangement so that his natural daughter by the second Duchess of Marlborough received his small fortune, without uncovering the nature of the kinship. See, *William Congreve: Letters and Documents*, ed. J. C. Hodges (1964), pp. 249–52.

[23] Hodges, *William Congreve the Man*, pp. 40, 51–2, 60–61.

[24] Letter to Earl of Manchester, *The Complete Works of Sir John Vanbrugh*, ed. B. Dobrée and G. Webb, vol. IV, p. 4.

ton and Congreve needed, but neither was it the failure which tradition once supposed. Emmett L. Avery[25], has concluded that the comedy rose from a "cool initial reception to considerable popularity" during the eighteenth century. Little performed in the first two decades of the century, it reached a point towards the end of the century when it was the most frequently performed of Congreve's plays.[26]

[25] Emmett L. Avery, *Congreve's Plays on the Eighteenth Century Stage* (1951), pp. 32–3.
[26] Avery, *op. cit.*, p. 155.

A NOTE ON THE TEXT

The Way of the World sets no complicated problems of transmission or priority. The four texts published by Jacob Tonson during the author's lifetime bear authority; the first and second editions of 1700 and 1706, and the first and "third" editions of *The Works of Mr. William Congreve*, published in 1710 (re-issued in 1717 as the "second" edition) and 1719–20. Congreve's textual revisions and alterations in these editions correct obvious errors, make minor stylistic changes, or alterations aiming at greater clarity. Other editions can be ignored; the pirated version which occurs in *Five Plays Written by Mr. Congreve* (1710, re-issued 1712), the 12mo edition of 1710, and that in volume VII of *A Collection of the Best English Plays* (1711 ff.) have no authority.

The most informative change which Congreve introduced was not substantive, but involved the typographical arrangement of the scenes. In both the first and second quarto editions the scene changed only when the setting shifted, like the overwhelming majority of seventeenth-century English plays. When Congreve's plays were reprinted in the three-volume collection of *The Works* in 1710, they appeared in a new guise. As in contemporary French printing practice, a new scene is numbered on every occasion that a character enters or leaves the stage, all exits and entrances are omitted, and the names of all the characters present given in capitals at the head of each scene. The 1719–20 edition of *The Works* moves even closer in appearance to French practice, for it centres the names of the speakers in small capitals above every speech.

There is no real doubt that Congreve was responsible for this change of style. When Jacob Tonson's nephew planned to reprint *The Works* shortly after Congreve's death, his uncle advised him to follow the 1710 edition, since Congreve "... took a great deal of care himself in the 8° edition I printed."[1]

At first glance, the re-styling of the layout looks like a clever piece

[1] *William Congreve: Letters and Documents* ed. J. C. Hodges, New York 1964, p. 148.

of typographical design aimed more at merchandising than clarity.
But it is not Francophile modishness which lies behind Congreve's
adoption of this eccentric pattern. John Dennis was always ready,
unlike the more reserved Congreve, to instruct his reader in literary
theory, and he gives the rationale for setting out his *Liberty Asserted*
(1704) in the same manner:

> ... here by the word Scene, I do not mean so much the Place, as
> the Number of Persons who are in Action upon that place at a time.
> I have therefore distinguished the Scenes ... as they have always
> been distinguish'd by the Ancients and by the Moderns of other
> Countries, and by our own *Ben. Johnson*. Any Person who comes
> upon the Place of Action, or leaves it, makes a different Scene, and
> that new Scene is mark'd by the Figure of its respective Number,
> and the Names of the Persons who are upon the Place of Action.
> I thought that agreeable Delusion into which the Reader willingly
> and gladly enters, for the sake of his Pleasure, would be both
> greater and easier if he were not put in mind of a Stage by *Entrances*
> and *Exits*, which are nothing but Directions that are given to a Play
> House Prompter ...[2].

To this statement may be added that of Laurence Echard, who followed
this pattern in his translation of Plautus in 1694, "I have all the way
divided the *Acts* and *Scenes* according to the true Rules of the
Stage ..."[3].

Congreve's division of the scenes in 1710 has, therefore, a dual
intention. First, *The Works* were to be the author's definitive reading
edition for posterity, cleared of as much of the impedimenta of stage
directions as was possible. Secondly, the very arrangement is a discreet
claim that the plays follow the "true Rules of the [neoclassical] Stage",
that is, they are "regular", obey the unities, and preserve the *liaisons
des scènes*. The neoclassical dress of *The Way of the World* points not
only to French, but also to Ben Jonson's classicism, and, ultimately,
to the great exemplars of Classical comedy, Plautus and Terence (and

[2] *The Critical Works of John Dennis*, ed. E. N. Hooker, I, pp. 323–324. Balti-
more, Md. (Johns Hopkins) 1939–43. See Hooker's note (*op. cit.*, p. 506) on this
passage.
[3] *Plautus's Comedies ... Made English* (1694), sig. b2ᵛ, reprinted by Augustan
Reprint Society, No. 129. Los Angeles 1968. Congreve owned a copy of this book.

in the Dedication Congreve makes his bow to the Roman dramatists). If further indication were necessary, Congreve signalled *The Way of the World*'s obedience to the unity of time by the note beneath the Personæ Dramatis, "*The Time equal to that of the Presentation.*"

Apart from this revealing change in lay-out, *The Way of the World* underwent three successive authorial revisions. The second quarto edition of 1706 corrects some misprints, alters the capitalisation, and changes some spellings. More important, punctuation differs on occasions, sometimes supplying a better reading, and there are some omissions or alterations for stylistic reasons (*e.g.* at II. I. 351–2, III. I. 69, 154, 163, 219–20, IV. I. 191, 542, V. I. 89, etc.).[4]

The 1710 edition takes this process further, and there is every sign that Congreve went over the text with the care Tonson claimed. On one occasion the rearrangement for the "reading edition" makes nonsense of the stage action—where in the first edition Lady Wishfort tells Betty to go out in the middle of her speech, the 1710 edition shifts the command, "Go you Thing and let her in", to the end of Lady Wishfort's speech, so that Betty has no sooner received the command than she lets Foible in (III. I. 58, 63). A reverse process may have been at work at V. I. 321, where an effort to make the action clearer to a reader may recall a piece of contemporary stage business (see textual note). Most of the changes, however, are made for stylistic reasons or for clarity (*e.g.* I. I. 76–7, 90, 130, 367, II. I. 18, 145, 309, III. I. 270, 388, IV. I. 189, 243, 309, V. I. 89, etc.).

Congreve's final tinkering with his text was in preparation for the 1719–20 edition of *The Works*, "Revis'd by the AUTHOR" according to the title-page. The Preface (by Congreve or Tonson) announces, "This edition . . . is only recommended as the least faulty Impression which has yet been Printed; in which, Care has been taken both to Revise the Press, and to Review and Correct Many Passages in the Writing" (vol. I, sig. A3–3ᵛ). In the case of *The Way of the World* a few passages are altered (and one of these, the transposition of phrases at I. I. 258–9, may be compositorial rather than the author's intention). Further alterations are introduced in punctuation, especially in the use of exclamation marks, and in other accidentals.

This edition is based on the first "stage" edition of 1700, as being the text closest to the comedy seen by the original audience in March

[4] The 1706 edition also introduces an error, "I do not now" for "I do now" (II. I. 127), which is perpetuated in the later texts.

1700. The Brotherton Library copy has been used as copy-text, and checked against the two copies in the Bodleian Library (Holkham d. 6, Malone 136 [5]), the copy in the Worcester College Library, and the British Museum copies (Ashley 2194, 841. c. 19, and 841. c. 9[8]). There are few press variants in the first edition. In one of the Bodleian Library copies (Holkham d. 6) the spaces between the words "as strange", "bred as", and "were not" have dropped out (IV. I. 193–4); but only one, the Worcester College copy, exhibits any real signs of alteration made during printing—where the Personæ Dramatis in the other copies reads simply "WOMEN.", the Worcester College copy reads "WOMEN. By"

A few obvious misprints have been corrected silently, such as "*Wtiwoud*" (II. I. 360), "ro" for "to" (V. I. 401), and "rcturn" for "return" (V. I. 325).). Names of characters are printed in large and small capitals in standardised forms in all stage directions and speech prefixes, except in the Personæ Dramatis where the conventions of the original copy are followed. Brackets have been silently removed from original stage directions and the punctuation normalised. All entrances have been ranged left, and all exits and other stage directions ranged to the right except where Congreve gives a detail of stage action in mid-speech. These directions to the actor have been put within square brackets (as "[hiccup]" at IV. i. 410), and on occasions shifted in the interest of clarity. The frequently irregular use of roman or italic punctuation in the quarto has been standardised, and the Prologue and Epilogue printed in roman instead of italic type. All other deviations from the copy-text are recorded in the Textual Notes and editorial additions to the stage directions placed within angle brackets.

Wherever possible, the reading of the first edition (Q1) has been preserved. On some occasions, punctuation and substantive readings have been taken from later editions where these texts correct Q1. The weight of emendations based on Q2 are of punctuation, but the 1710 *Works* (W1) provides rather more substantive corrections (*e.g.* "frailties" for "frailty's" at V. I. 116 comes from Q2, "we'll" for "will" at II. I. 236, "the" for "your" at V. I. 17, etc., from W1). Although the 1719–20 edition (W2) improves the punctuation and introduces one or two new readings, only one change, and that of punctuation (III. I. 502–3), has been made on the basis of this, the final authorial text. In one or two instances, a later spelling or punctuation has been preferred in the interest of clarity—therefore, at II. I. 421 and V. I. 221,

Q2's "than" is adopted in preference to Q1's "then" since the modern reader might be confused, and "Chery–" (Q1) at III. I. 21 is replaced by "Cherry–" (Q2). One emendation of punctuation not authorised by any later edition has been made (V. I. 97), following the example of Herbert Davis.

Clearly any text of *The Way of the World* based on the first quarto edition differs in important ways from the version which Congreve wished posterity to read. A strict adherence to the belief that the last edition revised during the author's lifetime should be the basis of a critical text, would argue for the primacy of the W2 text. Consequently, the textual notes to this edition are rather more elaborate than those given for most other plays in this series. The critical apparatus records not only editorial departures from the copy-text, but also gives the substantive variants from later editions overseen by Congreve, including punctuation where it affects meaning. This will enable the reader to follow Congreve's careful, often minute, revisions for his "reading edition".

No attempt has been made to record the alterations in typographical lay-out unless there is a change in stage directions, or unless evidence from later editions clarifies the placing of stage directions (*e.g.* III. I. 296). The most easily available reprint of the arrangement adopted by the 1710 edition is Bonamy Dobrée's edition of *The Comedies of William Congreve*, first published in the World's Classics in 1925.

PERSONÆ DRAMATIS

MEN.		By
Fainall,	In Love with *Mrs*. Marwood.	Mr. *Betterton*.
Mirabell,	In Love with *Mrs*. Millamant.	Mr. *Verbrugen*.
Witwoud, *Petulant*,	Followers of *Mrs*. Millamant.	Mr. *Bowen*. Mr. *Bowman*.
Sir *Willfull* *Witwoud*,	Half Brother to *Witwoud*, and Nephew to Lady *Wishfort*.	Mr. *Underhill*.
Waitwell,	Servant to *Mirabell*.	Mr. *Bright*.

WOMEN.		By
Lady *Wishfort*,	Enemy to *Mirabell*, for having falsely pretended Love to her.	Mrs. *Leigh*.
Mrs. *Millamant*,	A fine Lady, Niece to Lady *Wishfort*, and loves *Mirabell*.	Mrs. *Bracegirdle*.
Mrs. *Marwood*,	Friend to *Mr*. Fainall, and likes *Mirabell*.	Mrs. *Barry*.
Mrs. *Fainall*,	Daughter to Lady *Wishfort*, and Wife to *Fainall*, formerly Friend to *Mirabell*.	Mrs. *Bowman*.
Foible,	Woman to Lady *Wishfort*.	Mrs. *Willis*.
Mincing,	Woman to *Mrs*. Millamant.	Mrs. *Prince*.

Dancers, Footmen, *and* Attendants.

SCENE *LONDON*.

The Time equal to that of the Presentation.

My LORD,

Whether the World will arraign me of Vanity, or not, that I have presum'd to Dedicate this Comedy to your Lordship, I am yet in doubt: Tho' it may be it is some degree of Vanity even to doubt of it. One who has at any time had the Honour of your Lordship's 5
Conversation, cannot be suppos'd to think very meanly of that which he would prefer to your Perusal: Yet it were to incur the Imputation of too much Sufficiency, to pretend to such a Merit as might abide the Test of your Lordship's Censure.

Whatever Value may be wanting to this Play while yet it is mine, 10
will be sufficiently made up to it, when it is once become your Lordship's; and it is my Security, that I cannot have over-rated it more by my Dedication, than your Lordship will dignifie it by your Patronage.

That it succeeded on the Stage, was almost beyond my Expecta- 15
tion; for but little of it was prepar'd for that general Taste which seems now to be predominant in the Pallats of our Audience.

Those Characters which are meant to be ridiculous in most of our Comedies, are of Fools so gross, that in my humble Opinion, they should rather disturb than divert the well-natur'd and reflect- 20
ing part of an Audience; they are rather Objects of Charity than Contempt; and instead of moving our Mirth, they ought very often to excite our Compassion.

This Reflection mov'd me to design some Characters, which should appear ridiculous not so much thro' a natural Folly (which 25
is incorrigible, and therefore not proper for the Stage) as thro' an affected Wit; a Wit, which at the same time that it is affected, is also false. As there is some Difficulty in the formation of a Character of this Nature, so there is some Hazard which attends the progress of

its Success, upon the Stage: For many come to a Play, so over-   30
charg'd with Criticism, that they very often let fly their Censure,
when through their rashness they have mistaken their Aim. This I
had occasion lately to observe: For this Play had been Acted two
or three Days, before some of these hasty Judges cou'd find the
leisure to distinguish betwixt the Character of a *Witwoud* and a   35
Truewit.

I must beg your Lordship's Pardon for this Digression from the
true Course of this Epistle; but that it may not seem altogether
impertinent, I beg, that I may plead the occasion of it, in part of that
Excuse of which I stand in need, for recommending this Comedy   40
to your Protection. It is only by the Countenance of your Lordship,
and the *Few* so qualified, that such who write with Care and Pains can
hope to be distinguish'd: For the Prostituted Name of *Poet* promis-
cuously levels all that bear it.

Terence, the most correct Writer in the World, had a *Scipio* and a   45
Lelius if not to assist him, at least to support him in his Reputation:
And notwithstanding his extraordinary Merit, it may be, their
Countenance was not more than necessary.

The Purity of his Stile, the Delicacy of his Turns, and the Justness of his Characters, were all of them Beauties, which the greater   50
part of his Audience were incapable of Tasting: Some of the coursest
Strokes of *Plautus*, so severely censured by *Horace*, were more
likely to affect the Multitude; such, who come with expectation to
Laugh out the last Act of a Play, and are better entertained with two
or three unseasonable Jests, than with the artful Solution of the *Fable*.   55

As *Terence* excell'd in his Performances, so had he great Advan-
tages to encourage his Undertakings; for he built most on the
Foundations of *Menander*: His Plots were generally modell'd, and
his Characters ready drawn to his Hand. He copied *Menander*; and
Menander had no less Light in the Formation of his Characters,   60
from the Observations of *Theophrastus*, of whom he was a Disciple;
and *Theophrastus* it is known was not only the Disciple, but the
immediate Successor of *Aristotle*, the first and greatest Judge of
Poetry. These were great Models to design by; and the further
Advantage which *Terence* possess'd, towards giving his Plays the   65
due Ornaments of Purity of Stile, and Justness of Manners, was not
less considerable, from the freedom of Conversation, which was
permitted him with *Lelius* and *Scipio*, two of the greatest and most

polite Men of his Age. And indeed, the Privilege of such a Conversation, is the only certain Means of attaining to the Perfection   70
of Dialogue.

If it has happened in any part of this Comedy, that I have gain'd a
Turn of Stile, or Expression more Correct, or at least more
Corrigible than in those which I have formerly written, I must,
with equal Pride and Gratitude, ascribe it to the Honour of your   75
Lordship's admitting me into your Conversation, and that of a
Society where every-body else was so well worthy of you, in your
Retirement last Summer from the Town: For it was immediately
after, that this Comedy was written. If I have fail'd in my Per-
formance, it is only to be regretted, where there were so many,   80
not inferiour either to a *Scipio* or a *Lelius*, that there should be one
wanting equal to the Capacity of a *Terence*.

If I am not mistaken, Poetry is almost the only Art, which has
not yet laid claim to your Lordship's Patronage. Architecture, and
Painting, to the great Honour of our Country, have flourish'd   85
under your Influence and Protection. In the mean time, Poetry, the
eldest Sister of all Arts, and Parent of most, seems to have resign'd
her Birth-right, by having neglected to pay her Duty to your Lordship; and by permitting others of a later Extraction, to prepossess
that Place in your Esteem, to which none can pretend a better Title.   90
Poetry, in its Nature, is sacred to the Good and Great; the relation
between them is reciprocal, and they are ever propitious to it. It is
the Privilege of Poetry to address to them, and it is their Prerogative
alone to give it Protection.

This receiv'd Maxim, is a general Apology for all Writers who   95
Consecrate their Labours to great Men: But I could wish at this
time, that this Address were exempted from the common pretence
of all Dedications; and that as I can distinguish your Lordship even
among the most Deserving, so this Offering might become remark-
able by some particular Instance of Respect, which shou'd assure   100
your Lordship, that I am, with all due Sense of your extream
Worthiness and Humanity,

My LORD,

Your Lordship's most obedient
and most oblig'd humble Servant,

Will. Congreve.

PROLOGUE.

Spoken by Mr. *Betterton.*

Of those few Fools, who with ill Stars are curs'd,
Sure scribbling Fools, call'd Poets, fare the worst.
For they're a sort of Fools which *Fortune* makes,
And after she has made 'em Fools, forsakes.
With *Nature*'s Oafs 'tis quite a diff'rent Case,   5
For *Fortune* favours all her *Idiot-Race*:
In her own Nest the *Cuckow-Eggs* we find,
O'er which she broods to hatch the *Changling-Kind*.
No Portion for her own she has to spare,
So much she doats on her adopted Care.   10
   Poets are Bubbles, by the Town drawn in,
Suffer'd at first some trifling Stakes to win:
But what unequal Hazards do they run!
Each time they write, they venture all they've won:
The 'Squire that's butter'd still, is sure to be undone.   15
This Author, heretofore, has found your Favour,
But pleads no Merit from his past Behaviour.
To build on that might prove a vain Presumption,
Should Grants to Poets made, admit Resumption:
And in *Parnassus* he must lose his Seat,   20
If that be found a forfeited Estate.
   He owns, with Toil, he wrought the following Scenes,
But if they're naught ne're spare him for his Pains:
Damn him the more; have no Commiseration
For Dulness on mature Deliberation.   25
He swears he'll not resent one hiss'd-off Scene,
Nor, like those peevish Wits, his Play maintain,
Who, to assert their Sense, your Taste arraign.
Some Plot we think he has, and some new Thought;
Some Humour too, no Farce; but that's a Fault.   30

Satire, he thinks, you ought not to expect,
For so Reform'd a Town, who dares Correct?
To please, this time, has been his sole Pretence,
He'll not instruct least it should give Offence.
Should he by chance a Knave or Fool expose,   35
That hurts none here, sure here are none of those.
In short, our Play, shall (with your leave to shew it)
Give you one Instance of a Passive Poet.
Who to your Judgments yields all Resignation;
So Save or Damn, after your own Discretion.   40

ACT 1

SCENE I

A Chocolate-house

MIRABELL *and* FAINALL (*Rising from Cards*). BETTY *waiting*.

MIRABELL.   You are a fortunate Man, Mr. *Fainall*.

FAINALL.   Have we done?

MIRABELL.   What you please. I'll play on to entertain you.

FAINALL.   No, I'll give you your Revenge another time, when
you are not so indifferent; you are thinking of something else   5
now, and play too negligently; the Coldness of a losing Gamester
lessens the Pleasure of the Winner: I'd no more play with a Man
that slighted his ill Fortune, than I'd make Love to a Woman who
undervalu'd the loss of her Reputation.

MIRABELL.   You have a Taste extreamly delicate, and are for   10
refining on your Pleasures.

FAINALL.   Prithee, why so reserv'd? Something has put you out
of Humour.

MIRABELL.   Not at all: I happen to be grave to day; and you are
gay; that's all.   15

FAINALL.   Confess, *Millamant* and you quarrell'd last Night,
after I left you; my fair Cousin has some Humours, that wou'd
tempt the patience of a Stoick. What, some Coxcomb came in,
and was well receiv'd by her, while you were by.

MIRABELL. *Witwoud* and *Petulant*; and what was worse, her 20
Aunt, your Wife's Mother, my evil Genius; or to sum up all in
her own Name, my old Lady *Wishfort* came in.——

FAINALL.   O there it is then——She has a lasting Passion for
you, and with Reason.——What, then my Wife was there?

MIRABELL.   Yes, and Mrs. *Marwood* and three or four more, 25
whom I never saw before; seeing me, they all put on their grave
Faces, whisper'd one another; then complain'd aloud of the
Vapours, and after fell into a profound Silence.

FAINALL.   They had a mind to be rid of you.

MIRABELL.   For which Reason I resolv'd not to stir. At last the 30
good old Lady broke thro' her painful Taciturnity, with an
Invective against long Visits. I would not have understood her,
but *Millamant* joining in the Argument, I rose and with a con-
strain'd Smile told her, I thought nothing was so easie as to know
when a Visit began to be troublesome; she redned and I withdrew, 35
without expecting her Reply.

FAINALL.   You were to blame to resent what she spoke only in
Compliance with her Aunt.

MIRABELL.   She is more Mistress of her self, than to be under the
necessity of such a resignation.   40

FAINALL.   What? tho' half her Fortune depends upon her marrying with my Lady's Approbation?

MIRABELL.   I was then in such a Humour, that I shou'd have
been better pleas'd if she had been less discreet.

FAINALL.   Now I remember, I wonder not they were weary of 45
you; last Night was one of their Cabal-nights; they have 'em
three times a Week, and meet by turns, at one another's Apart-
ments, where they come together like the Coroner's Inquest, to
sit upon the murder'd Reputations of the Week. You and I are
excluded; and it was once propos'd that all the Male Sex shou'd 50
be excepted; but somebody mov'd that to avoid Scandal there
might be one Man of the Community; upon which Motion
Witwoud and *Petulant* were enroll'd Members.

MIRABELL.   And who may have been the Foundress of this Sect?
My Lady *Wishfort*, I warrant, who publishes her Detestation of 55
Mankind; and full of the Vigour of Fifty five, declares for a Friend

and *Ratafia*; and let Posterity shift for it self, she'll breed no more.

FAINALL.   The discovery of your sham Addresses to her, to conceal your Love to her Niece, has provok'd this Separation: 60
Had you dissembl'd better, Things might have continu'd in the state of Nature.

MIRABELL.   I did as much as Man cou'd, with any reasonable Conscience; I proceeded to the very last Act of Flattery with her, and was guilty of a Song in her Commendation: Nay, I got 65
a Friend to put her into a Lampoon, and complement her with the Imputation of an Affair with a young Fellow, which I carry'd so far, that I told her the malicious Town took notice that she was grown fat of a suddain; and when she lay in of a Dropsie, persuaded her she was reported to be in Labour. The Devil's 70
in't, if an old Woman is to be flatter'd further, unless a Man shou'd endeavour downright personally to debauch her; and that my Virture forbad me. But for the discovery of that Amour, I am Indebted to your Friend, or your Wife's Friend Mrs. *Marwood*. 75

FAINALL.   What should provoke her to be your Enemy, without she has made you Advances, which you have slighted? Women do not easily forgive Omissions of that Nature.

MIRABELL.   She was always civil to me, till of late; I confess I am not one of those Coxcombs who are apt to interpret a 80
Woman's good Manners to her Prejudice; and think that she who does not refuse 'em every thing, can refuse 'em nothing.

FAINALL.   You are a gallant Man, *Mirabell*; and tho' you may have Cruelty enough, not to satisfie a Lady's longing; you have too much Generosity, not to be tender of her Honour. Yet you 85
speak with an Indifference which seems to be affected; and confesses you are conscious of a Negligence.

MIRABELL.   You pursue the Argument with a distrust that seems to be unaffected, and confesses you are conscious of a Concern for which the Lady is more indebted to you, than your Wife. 90

FAINALL.   Fie, fie Friend, if you grow Censorious I must leave you;——I'll look upon the Gamesters in the next Room.

MIRABELL.   Who are they?

FAINALL.   *Petulant* and *Witwoud*.——Bring me some Chocolate.
                                                                            Exit.

MIRABELL.   *Betty*, what says your Clock?   95
BETTY.   Turn'd of the last Canonical Hour, Sir.

Exit.

MIRABELL.   How pertinently the Jade answers me! Ha? almost
One a Clock! [*Looking on his Watch.*] O, y'are come——
Enter a SERVANT.

Well; is the grand Affair over? You have been something tedious.

SERVANT.   Sir, there's such Coupling at *Pancras*, that they stand   100
behind one another, as 'twere in a Country Dance. Ours was the
last Couple to lead up; and no hopes appearing of dispatch,
besides, the Parson growing hoarse, we were afraid his Lungs
would have fail'd before it came to our turn; so we drove round
to *Duke*'s *Place*; and there they were riveted in a trice.   105
MIRABELL.   So, so, you are sure they are Married.
SERVANT.   Married and Bedded, Sir: I am Witness.
MIRABELL.   Have you the Certificate?
SERVANT.   Here it is, Sir.
MIRABELL.   Has the Taylor brought *Waitwell*'s Cloaths home,   110
and the new Liveries?
SERVANT.   Yes, Sir.
MIRABELL.   That's well. Do you go home again, d'ee hear, and
adjourn the Consummation till farther Order; bid *Waitwell* shake
his Ears, and Dame *Partlet* rustle up her Feathers, and meet   115
me at One a Clock by *Rosamond*'s Pond; that I may see her
before she returns to her Lady; and as you tender your Ears be
secret.

Exit SERVANT.
Re-enter FAINALL.

FAINALL.   Joy of your Success, *Mirabell*; you look pleas'd.
MIRABELL.   Ay; I have been engag'd in a Matter of some sort of   120
Mirth, which is not yet ripe for discovery. I am glad this is not a
Cabal-night. I wonder, *Fainall*, that you who are Married, and
of Consequence should be discreet, will suffer your Wife to be
of such a Party.
FAINALL.   Faith, I am not Jealous. Besides, most who are   125
engag'd are Women and Relations; and for the Men, they are of a
Kind too Contemptible to give Scandal.

MIRABELL.   I am of another Opinion. The greater the Coxcomb,
always the more the Scandal: For a Woman who is not a Fool,
can have but one Reason for associating with a Man that is.   130

FAINALL.   Are you Jealous as often as you see *Witwoud* entertain'd by *Millamant?*

MIRABELL.   Of her Understanding I am, if not of her Person.

FAINALL.   You do her wrong; for to give her her Due, she has
Wit.   135

MIRABELL.   She has Beauty enough to make any Man think so;
and Complaisance enough not to contradict him who shall tell her
so.

FAINALL.   For a passionate Lover, methinks you are a Man
somewhat too discerning in the Failings of your Mistress.   140

MIRABELL.   And for a discerning Man, somewhat too passionate
a Lover; for I like her with all her Faults; nay, like her for her
Faults. Her Follies are so natural, or so artful, that they become
her; and those Affectations which in another Woman wou'd be
odious, serve but to make her more agreeable. I'll tell thee,   145
Fainall, she once us'd me with that Insolence, that in Revenge
I took her to pieces; sifted her and separated her Failings; I
study'd 'em, and got 'em by rote. The Catalogue was so large,
that I was not without hopes, one Day or other to hate her
heartily: To which end I so us'd my self to think of 'em, that at   150
length, contrary to my Design and Expectation, they gave me
every Hour less and less disturbance; 'till in a few Days it became
habitual to me, to remember 'em without being displeas'd. They
are now grown as familiar to me as my own Frailties; and in all
probability in a little time longer I shall like 'em as well.   155

FAINALL.   Marry her, marry her; be half as well acquainted with
her Charms, as you are with her Defects, and my Life on't, you
are your own Man again.

MIRABELL.   Say you so?

FAINALL.   I, I, I have Experience: I have a Wife, and so forth.   160

Enter MESSENGER.

MESSENGER.   Is one Squire *Witwoud* here?

BETTY.   Yes; what's your Business?

MESSENGER. I have a Letter for him, from his Brother Sir *Wilfull*, which I am charg'd to deliver into his own Hands.

BETTY. He's in the next Room, Friend——That way.   165

Exit MESSENGER.

MIRABELL. What, is the Chief of that Noble Family in Town, Sir *Wilfull Witwoud*?

FAINALL. He is expected to Day. Do you know him?

MIRABELL. I have seen him, he promises to be an extraordinary Person; I think you have the Honour to be related to him.   170

FAINALL. Yes; he is half Brother to this *Witwoud* by a former Wife, who was Sister to my Lady *Wishfort*, my Wife's Mother. If you marry *Millamant* you must call Cousins too.

MIRABELL. I had rather be his Relation than his Acquaintance.

FAINALL. He comes to Town in order to Equip himself for   175
Travel.

MIRABELL. For Travel! Why the Man that I mean is above Forty.

FAINALL. No matter for that; 'tis for the Honour of *England*, that all *Europe* should know we have Blockheads of all Ages.   180

MIRABELL. I wonder there is not an Act of Parliament to save the Credit of the Nation, and prohibit the Exportation of Fools.

FAINALL. By no means, 'tis better as 'tis; 'tis better to Trade with a little Loss, than to be quite eaten up, with being over-stock'd.   185

MIRABELL. Pray, are the Follies of this Knight-Errant, and those of the Squire his Brother, any thing related?

FAINALL. Not at all; *Witwoud* grows by the Knight, like a Medlar grafted on a Crab. One will melt in your Mouth, and t'other set Teeth on edge; one is all Pulp, and the other all Core.   190

MIRABELL. So one will be rotten before he be ripe, and the other will be rotten without ever being ripe at all.

FAINALL. Sir *Wilfull* is an odd mixture of Bashfulness and Obstinacy.——But when he's drunk, he's as loving as the Monster in the Tempest; and much after the same manner. To   195
give the t'other his due; he has something of good Nature, and does not always want Wit.

MIRABELL. Not always; but as often as his Memory fails him, and his common place of Comparisons. He is a Fool with a good

B

Memory, and some few Scraps of other Folks Wit. He is one   200
whose Conversation can never be approv'd, yet it is now and then
to be endur'd. He has indeed one good Quality, he is not Excep-
tious; for he so passionately affects the Reputation of understanding Raillery; that he will construe an Affront into a Jest; and
call downright Rudeness and ill language, Satyr and Fire.   205

FAINALL.   If you have a mind to finish his Picture; you have an
opportunity to do it at full length. Behold the Original.

Enter WITWOUD.

WITWOUD.   Afford me your Compassion, my Dears; pity me,
Fainall, Mirabell, pity me.

MIRABELL.   I do from my Soul.   210

FAINALL.   Why, what's the Matter?

WITWOUD.   No letters for me, Betty?

BETTY.   Did not the Messenger bring you one but now, Sir?

WITWOUD.   Ay, but no other?

BETTY.   No, Sir.   215

WITWOUD.   That's hard, that's very hard;——A Messenger, a
Mule, a Beast of Burden, he has brought me a Letter from the
Fool my Brother, as heavy as a Panegyrick in a Funeral Sermon,
or a Copy of Commendatory Verses from one Poet to another.
And what's worse, 'tis as sure a forerunner of the Author, as an 220
Epistle Dedicatory.

MIRABELL.   A Fool, and your Brother *Witwoud*!

WITWOUD.   Ay, ay, my half Brother. My half Brother he is, no
nearer upon Honour.

MIRABELL.   Then 'tis possible he may be but half a Fool.   225

WITWOUD.   Good, good *Mirabell, le Drole*! Good, good, hang
him, don't let's talk of him;——*Fainall*, how does your Lady?
Gad, I say any thing in the World to get this Fellow out of my
Head. I beg Pardon that I shou'd ask a Man of Pleasure, and the
Town, a Question at once so Forreign and Domestick. But I   230
Talk like an old Maid at a Marriage, I don't know what I say:
But she's the best Woman in the World.

FAINALL.   'Tis well you don't know what you say, or else your
Commendation wou'd go near to make me either Vain or Jealous.

WITWOUD.   No Man in Town lives well with a Wife but *Fainall*: 235
Your Judgment *Mirabell*.

MIRABELL.   You had better step and ask his Wife; if you wou'd be credibly inform'd.

WITWOUD.   *Mirabell.*

MIRABELL.   Ay.   240

WITWOUD.   My Dear, I ask ten thousand Pardons;——Gad I have forgot what I was going to say to you.

MIRABELL.   I thank you heartily, heartily.

WITWOUD.   No, but prithee excuse me,——my Memory is such a Memory.   245

MIRABELL.   Have a care of such Apologies, *Witwoud*;—for I never knew a Fool but he affected to complain, either of the Spleen or his Memory.

FAINALL.   What have you done with *Petulant?*

WITWOUD.   He's reckoning his Mony,——my Mony it was;—— 250 I have no Luck to Day.

FAINALL.   You may allow him to win of you at Play;—for you are sure to be too hard for him at Repartee: since you monopolize the Wit that is between you, the Fortune must be his of Course.

MIRABELL.   I don't find that *Petulant* confesses the Superiority 255 of Wit to be your Talent, *Witwoud.*

WITWOUD.   Come, come, you are malicious now, and wou'd breed Debates.——*Petulant's* my Friend, and a very honest Fellow, and a very pretty Fellow, and has a smattering——Faith and Troth a pretty deal of an odd sort of a small Wit: Nay, I'll 260 do him Justice. I'm his Friend, I won't wrong him neither—— And if he had but any Judgment in the World,——he wou'd not be altogether contemptible. Come, come, don't detract from the Merits of my Friend.

FAINALL.   You don't take your Friend to be overnicely bred. 265

WITWOUD.   No, no, hang him, the Rogue has no Manners at all, that I must own——No more breeding than a Bum-baily, that I grant you,——'Tis Pity faith; the Fellow has Fire and Life.

MIRABELL.   What, Courage?

WITWOUD.   Hum, faith I don't know as to that,——I can't say 270 as to that.——Yes, Faith, in a Controversie he'll contradict any Body.

MIRABELL.   Tho' 'twere a Man whom he fear'd, or a Woman whom he lov'd.

WITWOUD.   Well, well, he does not always think before he   275
speaks;——We have all our Failings; you're too hard upon
him, you are Faith. Let me excuse him,——I can defend most
of his Faults, except one or two; one he has, that's the Truth
on't, if he were my Brother, I cou'd not acquit him——That
indeed I cou'd wish were otherwise.   280

MIRABELL.   Ay marry, what's that, *Witwoud?*

WITWOUD.   O pardon me——Expose the Infirmities of my
Friend.——No, my Dear, excuse me there.

FAINALL.   What I warrant he's unsincere, or 'tis some such
Trifle.   285

WITWOUD.   No, no, what if he be? 'Tis no matter for that, his Wit
will excuse that: A Wit shou'd no more be sincere, than a Woman
constant; one argues a decay of Parts, as t'other of Beauty.

MIRABELL.   May be you think him too positive?

WITWOUD.   No, no, his being positive is an Incentive to Argu-   290
ment, and keeps up Conversation.

FAINALL.   Too Illiterate.

WITWOUD.   That! that's his Happiness——His want of Learning, gives him the more opportunities to shew his natural Parts.

MIRABELL.   He wants Words.   295

WITWOUD.   Ay; but I like him for that now; for his want of
Words gives me the pleasure very often to explain his meaning.

FAINALL.   He's Impudent.

WITWOUD.   No; that's not it.

MIRABELL.   Vain.   300

WITWOUD.   No.

MIRABELL.   What, he speaks unseasonable Truths sometimes,
because he has not Wit enough to invent an Evasion.

WITWOUD.   Truths! Ha, ha, ha! No, no, since you will have it,
——I mean he never speaks Truth at all,——that's all. He will   305
lie like a Chambermaid, or a Woman of Quality's Porter. Now
that is a Fault.

Enter COACHMAN.

COACHMAN.   Is Master *Petulant* here, Mistress?

BETTY.   Yes.

COACHMAN.   Three Gentlewomen in the Coach would speak   310
with him.

FAINALL.   O brave *Petulant*, three!
BETTY.   I'll tell him.
COACHMAN.   You must bring two Dishes of Chocolate and a
Glass of Cinnamon-water.   315

Exit ⟨BETTY *and* COACHMAN⟩.

WITWOUD.   That should be for two fasting Strumpets, and a
Bawd troubl'd with Wind. Now you may know what the three
are.
MIRABELL.   You are very free with your Friends Acquaintance.
WITWOUD.   Ay, ay, Friendship without Freedom is as dull as   320
Love without Enjoyment, or Wine without Toasting; but to
tell you a Secret, these are Trulls that he allows Coach-hire, and
something more by the Week, to call on him once a Day at pub-
lick Places.
MIRABELL.   How!   325
WITWOUD.   You shall see he won't go to 'em because there's no
more Company here to take notice of him——Why this is
nothing to what he us'd to do;——Before he found out this way,
I have known him call for himself——
FAINALL.   Call for himself? What dost thou mean?   330
WITWOUD.   Mean, why he wou'd slip you out of this Chocolate-
house, just when you have been talking to him——As soon as
your Back was turn'd——Whip he was gone;——Then trip to
his Lodging, clap on a Hood and Scarf, and Mask, slap into a
Hackney-Coach, and drive hither to the Door again in a trice;   335
where he wou'd send in for himself, that I mean, call for himself,
wait for himself, nay and what's more, not finding himself, sometimes leave a Letter for himself.
MIRABELL.   I confess this is something extraordinary——I
believe he waits for himself now, he is so long a coming; O I ask   340
his Pardon.

Enter PETULANT ⟨*and* BETTY⟩.

BETTY.   Sir, the Coach stays.
PETULANT.   Well, well; I come——Sbud, a Man had as good be
a profess'd Midwife as a profest Whoremaster, at this rate; to be
knock'd up and rais'd at all Hours, and in all Places. Pox on 'em   345

I won't come.——Dee hear, tell 'em I won't come.——Let 'em snivel and cry their Hearts out.

FAINALL.   You are very cruel, *Petulant*.

PETULANT.   All's one, let it pass——I have a Humour to be cruel.   350

MIRABELL.   I hope they are not Persons of Condition that you use at this rate.

PETULANT.   Condition, Condition's a dry'd Fig, if I am not in Humour——By this Hand, if they were your——a——a—— your What-dee-call-'ems themselves, they must wait or rub off,   355 if I want Appetite.

MIRABELL.   What-dee-call-'ems! What are they, *Witwoud*?

WITWOUD.   Empresses, my Dear——By your What-dee-call-'ems he means Sultana Queens.

PETULANT.   Ay, *Roxolana*'s.   360

MIRABELL.   Cry you Mercy.

FAINALL.   *Witwoud* says they are——

PETULANT.   What does he say th'are?

WITWOUD.   I; fine Ladies I say.

PETULANT.   Pass on, *Witwoud*——Hearkee, by this Light his   365 Relations——Two Coheiresses his Cousins, and an old Aunt, that loves Catterwauling better than a Conventicle.

WITWOUD.   Ha, ha, ha; I had a Mind to see how the Rogue wou'd come off——Ha, ha, ha; Gad I can't be angry with him; if he said they were my Mother and my Sisters.   370

MIRABELL.   No!

WITWOUD.   No; the Rogue's Wit and Readiness of Invention charm me, dear *Petulant*.

BETTY.   They are gone Sir, in great Anger.

PETULANT.   Enough, let 'em trundle. Anger helps Complexion,   375 saves Paint.

FAINALL.   This Continence is all dissembled; this is in order to have something to brag of the next time he makes Court to *Millamant*, and swear he has abandon'd the whole Sex for her Sake.   380

MIRABELL.   Have you not left off your impudent Pretensions there yet? I shall cut your Throat, sometime or other *Petulant*, about that Business.

PETULANT. Ay, ay, let that pass——There are other Throats
to be cut—— 385

MIRABELL. Meaning mine, Sir?

PETULANT. Not I——I mean no Body——I know nothing.
——But there are Uncles and Nephews in the World——And
they may be Rivals——What then? All's one for that——

MIRABELL. How! hearkee *Petulant*, come hither——Explain, 390
or I shall call your Interpreter.

PETULANT. Explain, I know nothing——Why you have an
Uncle, have you not, lately come to Town, and lodges by my
Lady *Wishfort*'s?

MIRABELL. True. 395

PETULANT. Why that's enough——You and he are not Friends;
and if he shou'd marry and have a Child, you may be disinherited,
ha?

MIRABELL. Where hast thou stumbled upon all this Truth?

PETULANT. All's one for that; why then say I know something. 400

MIRABELL. Come, thou art an honest Fellow *Petulant*, and shalt
make Love to my Mistress, thou sha't, Faith. What hast thou
heard of my Uncle?

PETULANT. I, nothing I. If Throats are to be cut, let Swords
clash; snugs the Word, I shrug and am silent. 405

MIRABELL. O Raillery, Raillery. Come, I know thou art in the
Women's Secrets——What you're a Cabalist, I know you staid
at *Millamant*'s last Night, after I went. Was there any mention
made of my Uncle, or me? Tell me; if thou hadst but good Nature
equal to thy Wit *Petulant*, *Tony Witwoud*, who is now thy Com- 410
petitor in Fame, wou'd shew as dim by thee as a dead Whiting's
Eye, by a Pearl of Orient; he wou'd no more be seen by thee, then
Mercury is by the Sun: Come, I'm sure thou wo't tell me.

PETULANT. If I do, will you grant me common Sense then, for
the future? 415

MIRABELL. Faith I'll do what I can for thee; and I'll pray that
Heav'n may grant it thee in the mean time.

PETULANT. Well, hearkee.

FAINALL. *Petulant* and you both will find *Mirabell* as warm a
Rival as a Lover. 420

WITWOUD. Pshaw, pshaw, that she laughs at *Petulant* is plain.
And for my part——But that it is almost a Fashion to admire her,

I shou'd——Hearkee——To tell you a Secret, but let it go no
further——Between Friends, I shall never break my Heart for
her.   425

FAINALL.   How!

WITWOUD.   She's handsome; but she's a sort of an uncertain
Woman.

FAINALL.   I thought you had dy'd for her.

WITWOUD.   Umh——No——   430

FAINALL.   She has Wit.

WITWOUD.   'Tis what she will hardly allow any Body else;——
Now, Demme, I shou'd hate that, if she were as handsome as
Cleopatra. Mirabell is not so sure of her as he thinks for.

FAINALL.   Why do you think so?   435

WITWOUD.   We staid pretty late there last Night; and heard
something of an Uncle to *Mirabell*, who is lately come to Town,
——and is between him and the best part of his Estate; *Mirabell*
and he are at some distance, as my Lady *Wishfort* has been told;
and you know she hates *Mirabell*, worse than a Quaker hates a   440
Parrot, or than a Fishmonger hates a hard Frost. Whether this
Uncle has seen Mrs. *Millamant* or not, I cannot say; but there were
Items of such a Treaty being in Embrio; and if it shou'd come to
Life; poor *Mirabell* wou'd be in some sort unfortunately fobb'd
ifaith.   445

FAINALL.   'Tis impossible *Millamant* should hearken to it.

WITWOUD.   Faith, my Dear, I can't tell; she's a Woman and a
kind of a Humorist.

MIRABELL.   And this is the Sum of what you cou'd collect last
Night.   450

PETULANT.   The Quintessence. May be *Witwoud* knows more, he
stay'd longer——Besides they never mind him; they say any
thing before him.

MIRABELL.   I thought you had been the greatest Favourite.

PETULANT.   Ay *teste a teste*; But not in publick, because I make   455
Remarks.

MIRABELL.   Do you.

PETULANT.   Ay, ay, pox I'm malicious, Man. Now he's soft you
know, they are not in awe of him——The Fellow's well bred,
he's what you call a——What-dee-call-'em. A fine Gentleman,   460
but he's silly withal.

MIRABELL. I thank you, I know as much as my Curiosity requires. *Fainall*, are you for the *Mall*?

FAINALL. Ay, I'll take a turn before Dinner.

WITWOUD. Ay, we'll all walk in the Park, the Ladies talk'd of 465 being there.

MIRABELL. I thought you were oblig'd to watch for your Brother Sir *Wilfull*'s arrival.

WITWOUD. No, no, he comes to his Aunts, my Lady *Wishfort*; pox on him, I shall be troubled with him too; what shall I do 470 with the Fool?

PETULANT. Beg him for his Estate; that I may beg you afterwards; and so have but one Trouble with you both.

WITWOUD. O rare *Petulant*; thou art as quick as a Fire in a frosty Morning; thou shalt to the *Mall* with us; and we'll be 475 very severe.

PETULANT. Enough, I'm in a Humour to be severe.

MIRABELL. Are you? Pray then walk by your selves,—— Let not us be accessary to your putting the Ladies out of Countenance, with your senseless Ribaldry; which you roar out 480 aloud as often as they pass by you; and when you have made a handsome Woman blush, then you think you have been severe.

PETULANT. What, what? Then let 'em either shew their Innocence by not understanding what they hear, or else shew their Discretion by not hearing what they would not be thought to 485 understand.

MIRABELL. But hast not thou then Sense enough to know that thou ought'st to be most asham'd thy Self, when thou hast put another out of Countenance.

PETULANT. Not I, by this Hand——I always take blushing 490 either for a Sign of Guilt, or ill Breeding.

MIRABELL. I confess you ought to think so. You are in the right, that you may plead the error of your Judgment in defence of your Practice.

> *Where Modesty's ill Manners, 'tis but fit* 495
> *That Impudence and Malice, pass for Wit.*

Exeunt.

ACT II

St James's Park

Enter MRS FAINALL *and* MRS MARWOOD.

MRS FAINALL.   Ay, ay, dear *Marwood*, if we will be happy, we
must find the means in our selves, and among our selves. Men
are ever in Extreams; either doating or averse. While they are
Lovers, if they have Fire and Sense, their Jealousies are insupportable: And when they cease to Love, (we ought to think   5
at least) they loath; they look upon us with Horror and Distaste;
they meet us like the Ghosts of what we were, and as such fly from
us.

MRS MARWOOD.   True, 'tis an unhappy Circumstance of Life,
that Love shou'd ever die before us; and that the Man so often   10
shou'd out-live the Lover. But say what you will, 'tis better to be
left, than never to have been lov'd. To pass our Youth in dull
Indifference, to refuse the Sweets of Life because they once must
leave us; is as preposterous, as to wish to have been born Old,
because we one Day must be Old. For my part, my Youth may   15
wear and waste, but it shall never rust in my Possession.

MRS FAINALL.   Then it seems you dissemble an Aversion to
Mankind, only in compliance with my Mothers Humour.

MRS MARWOOD.   Certainly. To be free; I have no Taste of
those insipid dry Discourses, with which our Sex of force must   20
entertain themselves, apart from Men. We may affect Endear-
ments to each other, profess eternal Friendships, and seem to doat
like Lovers; but 'tis not in our Natures long to persevere. Love
will resume his Empire in our Breasts, and every Heart, or soon or
late, receive and readmit him as its lawful Tyrant.   25

MRS FAINALL.   Bless me, how have I been deceiv'd! Why you
profess a Libertine.

MRS MARWOOD.   You see my Friendship by my Freedom.
Come, be as sincere, acknowledge that your Sentiments agree
with mine.   30

MRS FAINALL.   Never.

Mrs Marwood.   You hate Mankind?

Mrs Fainall.   Heartily, Inveterately.

Mrs Marwood.   Your Husband?

Mrs Fainall.   Most transcendantly; ay, tho' I say it, meri-   35
toriously.

Mrs Marwood.   Give me your Hand upon it.

Mrs Fainall.   There.

Mrs Marwood.   I join with you; what I have said, has been to
try you.   40

Mrs Fainall.   Is it possible? Dost thou hate those Vipers
Men?

Mrs Marwood.   I have done hating 'em; and am now come
to despise 'em; the next thing I have to do, is eternally to forget
'em.   45

Mrs Fainall.   There spoke the Spirit of an Amazon, a
Penthesilea.

Mrs Marwood.   And yet I am thinking sometimes, to carry
my Aversion further.

Mrs Fainall.   How?   50

Mrs Marwood.   Faith by Marrying; if I cou'd but find one
that lov'd me very well, and would be thoroughly sensible of ill
usage; I think I shou'd do my self the violence of undergoing the
Ceremony.

Mrs Fainall.   You would not make him a Cuckold?   55

Mrs Marwood.   No; but I'd make him believe I did, and that's
as bad.

Mrs Fainall.   Why, had not you as good do it?

Mrs Marwood.   O if he shou'd ever discover it, he wou'd then
know the worst; and be out of his Pain; but I wou'd have him   60
ever to continue upon the Rack of Fear and Jealousy.

Mrs Fainall.   Ingenious Mischief! Wou'd thou wert married
to *Mirabell*.

Mrs Marwood.   Wou'd I were.

Mrs Fainall.   You change Colour.   65

Mrs Marwood.   Because I hate him.

Mrs Fainall.   So do I; but I can hear him nam'd. But what
Reason have you to hate him in particular?

Mrs Marwood.   I never lov'd him; he is, and always was
insufferably proud.   70

MRS FAINALL.   By the Reason you give for your Aversion, one
wou'd think it dissembl'd; for you have laid a Fault to his Charge,
of which his Enemies must acquit him.

MRS MARWOOD.   O then it seems you are one of his favourable
Enemies. Methinks you look a little pale, and now you flush   75
again.

MRS FAINALL.   Do I? I think I am a little sick o' the suddain.

MRS MARWOOD.   What ails you?

MRS FAINALL.   My Husband. Don't you see him? He turn'd   80
short upon me unawares, and has almost overcome me.

Enter FAINALL *and* MIRABELL.

MRS MARWOOD.   Ha, ha, ha; he comes opportunely for you.

MRS FAINALL.   For you, for he has brought *Mirabell* with him.

FAINALL.   My Dear.

MRS FAINALL.   My Soul.   85

FAINALL.   You don't look well to Day, Child.

MRS FAINALL.   Dee think so?

MIRABELL.   He is the only Man that do's, Madam.

MRS FAINALL.   The only Man that would tell me so at least;
and the only Man from whom I could hear it without Mortifica-   90
tion.

FAINALL.   O my Dear I am satisfy'd of your Tenderness; I know
you cannot resent any thing from me; especially what is an effect
of my Concern.

MRS FAINALL.   Mr. *Mirabell*; my Mother interrupted you in a 95
pleasant Relation last Night: I wou'd fain hear it out.

MIRABELL.   The Persons concern'd in that Affair, have yet a
tollerable Reputation——I am afraid Mr. *Fainall* will be Censorious.

MRS FAINALL.   He has a Humour more prevailing than his   100
Curiosity, and will willingly dispence with the hearing of one
scandalous Story; to avoid giving an occasion to make another
by being seen to walk with his Wife. This way Mr. *Mirabell*, and
I dare promise you will oblige us both.

Exeunt MRS FAINALL *and* MIRABELL.

FAINALL.   Excellent Creature! Well sure if I shou'd live to be 105
rid of my Wife, I shou'd be a miserable Man.

MRS MARWOOD. Ay!

FAINALL. For having only that one Hope, the accomplishment of it, of Consequence must put an end to all my hopes; and what a Wretch is he who must survive his hopes! Nothing remains when that Day comes, but to sit down and weep like *Alexander*, when he wanted other Worlds to conquer.

MRS MARWOOD. Will you not follow 'em?

FAINALL. Faith, I think not.

MRS MARWOOD. Pray let us; I have a Reason.

FAINALL. You are not Jealous?

MRS MARWOOD. Of whom?

FAINALL. Of *Mirabell*.

MRS MARWOOD. If I am, is it inconsistent with my Love to you that I am tender of your Honour?

FAINALL. You wou'd intimate then, as if there were a *fellow-feeling* between my Wife and Him.

MRS MARWOOD. I think she do's not hate him to that degree she wou'd be thought.

FAINALL. But he, I fear, is too Insensible.

MRS MARWOOD. It may be you are deceiv'd.

FAINALL. It may be so. I do now begin to apprehend it.

MRS MARWOOD. What?

FAINALL. That I have been deceiv'd Madam, and you are false.

MRS MARWOOD. That I am false! What mean you?

FAINALL. To let you know I see through all your little Arts—— Come, you both love him; and both have equally dissembl'd your Aversion. Your mutual Jealousies of one another, have made you clash till you have both struck Fire. I have seen the warm Confession red'ning on your Cheeks, and sparkling from your Eyes.

MRS MARWOOD. You do me wrong.

FAINALL. I do not——'Twas for my ease to oversee and wilfully neglect the gross advances made him by my Wife; that by permitting her to be engag'd, I might continue unsuspected in my Pleasures; and take you oftner to my Arms in full Security. But cou'd you think because the nodding Husband would not wake, that e'er the watchful Lover slept!

MRS MARWOOD. And wherewithal can you reproach me?

FAINALL.   With Infidelity, with loving of another, with love of   145
Mirabell.

MRS MARWOOD.   'Tis false. I challenge you to shew an Instance
that can confirm your groundless Accusation. I hate him.

FAINALL.   And wherefore do you hate him? He is Insensible, and
your Resentment follows his Neglect. An Instance? The Injuries   150
you have done him are a proof: Your interposing in his Love.
What cause had you to make Discoveries of his pretended
Passion? To undeceive the credulous Aunt, and be the officious
Obstacle of his Match with *Millamant*?

MRS MARWOOD.   My Obligations to my Lady urg'd me: I had   155
profess'd a Friendship to her; and could not see her easie Nature
so abus'd by that Dissembler.

FAINALL.   What, was it Conscience then! profess'd a Friendship!
O the pious Friendships of the Female Sex!

MRS MARWOOD.   More tender, more sincere, and more endur-   160
ing, than all the vain and empty Vows of Men, whether professing
Love to us, or mutual Faith to one another.

FAINALL.   Ha, ha, ha; you are my Wife's Friend too.

MRS MARWOOD.   Shame and Ingratitude! Do you reproach me?
You, you upbraid me! Have I been false to her, thro' strict   165
Fidelity to you, and sacrific'd my Friendship to keep my Love
inviolate? And have you the baseness to charge me with the
Guilt, unmindful of the Merit! To you it shou'd be meritorious,
that I have been vicious. And do you reflect that Guilt upon me,
which should lie buried in your Bosom?   170

FAINALL.   You misinterpret my Reproof. I meant but to remind
you of the slight Account you once could make of strictest Ties,
when set in Competition with your Love to me.

MRS MARWOOD.   'Tis false, you urg'd it with deliberate
Malice——'Twas spoke in scorn, and I never will forgive it.   175

FAINALL.   Your Guilt, not your Resentment, begets your Rage.
If yet you lov'd, you could forgive a Jealousy: But you are stung
to find you are discover'd.

MRS MARWOOD.   It shall be all discover'd. You too shall be
discover'd; be sure you shall. I can but be expos'd——If I do it   180
my self I shall prevent your Baseness.

FAINALL.   Why, what will you do?

MRS MARWOOD.   Disclose it to your Wife; own what has past
between us.

FAINALL.   Frenzy!   185

MRS MARWOOD.   By all my Wrongs I'll do't——I'll publish to
the World the Injuries you have done me, both in my Fame and
Fortune: With both I trusted you, you Bankrupt in Honour, as
indigent of Wealth.

FAINALL.   Your Fame I have preserv'd. Your Fortune has been   190
bestow'd as the prodigality of your Love would have it, in
Pleasures which we both have shar'd. Yet had not you been false,
I had e'er this repaid it——'Tis true——Had you permitted
Mirabell with *Millamant* to have stoll'n their Marriage, my Lady
had been incens'd beyond all means of reconcilement: *Millamant*   195
had forfeited the Moiety of her Fortune; which then wou'd have
descended to my Wife;——And wherefore did I marry, but to
make lawful Prize of a rich Widow's Wealth, and squander it on
Love and you?

MRS MARWOOD.   Deceit and frivolous Pretence.   200

FAINALL.   Death, am I not married? what's pretence? Am I not
Imprison'd, Fetter'd? Have I not a Wife? Nay a Wife that was a
Widow, a young Widow, a handsome Widow; and would be
again a Widow, but that I have a Heart of Proof, and something
of a Constitution to bustle thro' the ways of Wedlock and this   205
World. Will you yet be reconcil'd to Truth and me?

MRS MARWOOD.   Impossible. Truth and you are inconsistent
——I hate you, and shall for ever.

FAINALL.   For loving you?

MRS MARWOOD.   I loath the name of Love after such usage; and   210
next to the Guilt with which you wou'd asperse me, I scorn you
most. Farewell.

FAINALL.   Nay, we must not part thus.

MRS MARWOOD.   Let me go.

FAINALL.   Come, I'm sorry.   215

MRS MARWOOD.   I care not——Let me go——Break my
Hands, do——I'd leave 'em to get loose.

FAINALL.   I would not hurt you for the World. Have I no other
Hold to keep you here?

MRS MARWOOD.   Well, I have deserv'd it all.   220

FAINALL.   You know I love you.

MRS MARWOOD.   Poor dissembling!——O that——Well, it is
not yet——

FAINALL.   What? what is it not? What is it not yet? It is not yet
too late——   225

MRS MARWOOD.   No, it is not yet too late——I have that
Comfort.

FAINALL.   It is to love another.

MRS MARWOOD.   But not to loath, detest, abhor Mankind, my
self and the whole treacherous World.   230

FAINALL.   Nay, this is Extravagance——Come I ask your
Pardon——No Tears——I was to blame, I cou'd not love you
and be easie in my Doubts——Pray forbear——I believe you;
I'm convinc'd I've done you wrong; and any way, every way
will make amends;——I'll hate my Wife yet more, Dam her, I'll   235
part with her, rob her of all she's worth, and we'll retire somewhere, any where, to another World, I'll marry thee——Be
pacify'd——'Sdeath they come, hide your Face, your Tears——
You have a Mask, wear it a Moment. This way, this way, be
persuaded.   240

Exeunt.

Enter MIRABELL *and* MRS FAINALL.

MRS FAINALL.   They are here yet.

MIRABELL.   They are turning into the other Walk.

MRS FAINALL.   While I only hated my Husband, I could bear
to see him; but since I have despis'd him, he's too offensive.

MIRABELL.   O you should Hate with Prudence.   245

MRS FAINALL.   Yes, for I have Lov'd with Indiscretion.

MIRABELL.   You shou'd have just so much disgust for your
Husband, as may be suffiicent to make you relish your Lover.

MRS FAINALL.   You have been the cause that I have lov'd without Bounds, and wou'd you set Limits to that Aversion, of which   250
you have been the occasion? Why did you make me marry this
Man?

MIRABELL.   Why do we daily commit disagreeable and dangerous
Actions? To save that Idol Reputation. If the familiarities of our
Loves had produc'd that Consequence, of which you were appre-   255
hensive, Where could you have fix'd a Father's Name with
Credit, but on a Husband? I knew *Fainall* to be a Man lavish of

his Morals, an interested and professing Friend, a false and design-
ing Lover; yet one whose Wit and outward fair Behaviour, have
gain'd a Reputation with the Town, enough to make that Woman 260
stand excus'd, who has suffer'd herself to be won by his
Addresses. A better Man ought not to have been sacrific'd to the
Occasion; a worse had not answer'd to the Purpose. When you
are weary of him, you know your Remedy.

MRS FAINALL. I ought to stand in some degree of Credit with 265
you, *Mirabell*.

MIRABELL. In Justice to you, I have made you privy to my
whole Design, and put it in your Power to ruin or advance my
Fortune.

MRS FAINALL. Whom have you instructed to represent your 270
pretended Uncle?

MIRABELL. *Waitwell*, my Servant.

MRS FAINALL. He is an humble Servant to *Foible* my Mothers
Woman; and may win her to your Interest.

MIRABELL. Care is taken for that——She is won and worn by 275
this time. They were married this morning.

MRS FAINALL. Who?

MIRABELL. *Waitwell* and *Foible*. I wou'd not tempt my Servant
to betray me by trusting him too far. If your Mother, in hopes to
ruin me, shou'd consent to marry my pretended Uncle, he might 280
like *Mosca* in the *Fox*, stand upon Terms; so I made him sure
before-hand.

MRS FAINALL. So, if my poor Mother is caught in a Contract,
you will discover the Imposture betimes; and release her by
producing a Certificate of her Gallants former Marriage. 285

MIRABELL. Yes, upon Condition she consent to my Marriage
with her Niece, and surrender the Moiety of her Fortune in her
Possession.

MRS FAINALL. She talk'd last Night of endeavouring at a
Match between *Millamant* and your Uncle. 290

MIRABELL. That was by *Foible*'s Direction, and my Instruction,
that she might seem to carry it more privately.

MRS FAINALL. Well, I have an Opinion of your Success; for I
believe my Lady will do any thing to get a Husband; and when
she has this, which you have provided for her, I suppose she will 295
submit to any thing to get rid of him.

MIRABELL.   Yes, I think the good Lady wou'd marry any Thing that resembl'd a Man, tho' 'twere no more than what a Butler cou'd pinch out of a Napkin.

MRS FAINALL.   Female Frailty! We must all come to it, if we live to be Old and feel the craving of a false Appetite when the true is decay'd.   300

MIRABELL.   An old Woman's Appetite is deprav'd like that of a Girl——'Tis the Green Sickness of a second Childhood; and like the faint Offer of a latter Spring, serves but to usher in the Fall; and withers in an affected Bloom.   305

MRS FAINALL.   Here's your Mistress.

Enter MRS MILLAMANT, WITWOUD, *and* MINCING.

MIRABELL.   Here she comes Ifaith full sail, with her Fan spread and her Streamers out, and a shoal of Fools for Tenders——Ha, no, I cry her Mercy.   310

MRS FAINALL.   I see but one poor empty Sculler; and he tows her Woman after him.

MIRABELL.   You seem to be unattended, Madam——You us'd to have the *Beau-mond* Throng after you; and a Flock of gay fine Perrukes hovering round you.   315

WITWOUD.   Like Moths about a Candle——I had like to have lost my Comparison for want of Breath.

MILLAMANT.   O I have deny'd my self Airs to Day. I have walk'd as fast through the Crowd——

WITWOUD.   As a Favourite in disgrace; and with as few Followers.   320

MILLAMANT.   Dear Mr. *Witwoud*, truce with your Similitudes: For I am as sick of 'em——

WITWOUD.   As a Phisician of a good Air——I cannot help it Madam, tho' 'tis against my self.   325

MILLAMANT.   Yet again! *Mincing*, stand between me and his Wit.

WITWOUD.   Do Mrs. *Mincing*, like a Skreen before a great Fire. I confess I do blaze to Day, I am too bright.

MRS FAINALL.   But dear *Millamant*, why were you so long?   330

MILLAMANT.   Long! Lord, have I not made violent haste? I have ask'd every living Thing I met for you; I have enquir'd after you, as after a new Fashion.

WITWOUD.   Madam, truce with your Similitudes——No, you
met her Husband and did not ask him for her.   335

MIRABELL.   By your leave *Witwoud*, that were like enquiring after
an old Fashion, to ask a Husband for his Wife.

WITWOUD.   Hum, a hit, a hit, a palpable hit, I confess it.

MRS FAINALL.   You were dress'd before I came abroad.

MILLAMANT.   Ay, that's true——O but then I had——*Mincing*   340
what had I? Why was I so long?

MINCING.   O Mem, your Laship staid to peruse a Pecquet of
Letters.

MILLAMANT.   O ay, Letters——I had Letters——I am per-
secuted with Letters——I hate Letters——No Body knows how   345
to write Letters; and yet one has 'em, one does not know why
——They serve one to pin up one's Hair.

WITWOUD.   Is that the way? Pray Madam, do you pin up your
Hair with all your Letters? I find I must keep Copies.

MILLAMANT.   Only with those in Verse, Mr. *Witwoud*. I never pin   350
up my Hair with Prose. I fancy ones Hair wou'd not curl if it were
pinn'd up with Prose. I think I try'd once *Mincing*.

MINCING.   O Mem, I shall never forget it.

MILLAMANT.   Ay, poor *Mincing* tift and tift all the morning.

MINCING.   'Till I had the Cremp in my Fingers I'll vow Mem.   355
And all to no purpose. But when your Laship pins it up with
Poetry, it sits so pleasant the next Day as any Thing, and is so
pure and so crips.

WITWOUD.   Indeed, so crips?

MINCING.   You're such a Critick, Mr. *Witwoud*.   360

MILLAMANT.   *Mirabell*, Did not you take Exceptions last Night?
O ay, and went away——Now I think on't I'm angry——No,
now I think on't I'm pleas'd——For I believe I gave you some
Pain.

MIRABELL.   Do's that please you?   365

MILLAMANT.   Infinitely; I love to give Pain.

MIRABELL.   You wou'd affect a Cruelty which is not in your
Nature; your true Vanity is in the power of pleasing.

MILLAMANT.   O I ask your Pardon for that——One's Cruelty
is one's Power, and when one parts with one's Cruelty, one parts   370
with one's Power; and when one has parted with that, I fancy
one's Old and Ugly.

MIRABELL.   Ay, ay, suffer your Cruelty to ruin the object of
your Power, to destroy your Lover——And then how vain, how
lost a Thing you'll be! Nay, 'tis true: You are no longer handsome   375
when you've lost your Lover; your Beauty dies upon the Instant:
For Beauty is the Lovers Gift; 'tis he bestows your Charms——
Your Glass is all a Cheat. The Ugly and the Old, whom the
Looking-glass mortifies, yet after Commendation can be
flatter'd by it, and discover Beauties in it: For that reflects our   380
Praises, rather than your Face.

MILLAMANT.   O the Vanity of these Men! *Fainall*, dee hear him?
If they did not commend us, we were not handsome! Now you
must know they could not commend one, if one was not handsome. Beauty the Lover's Gift——Lord, what is a Lover, that   385
it can give? Why one makes Lovers as fast as one pleases, and
they live as long as one pleases, and they die as soon as one
pleases: And then if one pleases, one makes more.

WITWOUD.   Very pretty. Why you make no more of making of
Lovers, Madam, than of making so many Card-matches.   390

MILLAMANT.   One no more owes one's Beauty to a Lover, than
ones Wit to an Eccho: They can but reflect what we look and say;
vain empty Things if we are silent or unseen, and want a being.

MIRABELL.   Yet to those two vain empty Things, you owe two
the greatest Pleasures of your Life.   395

MILLAMANT.   How so?

MIRABELL.   To your Lover you owe the pleasure of hearing your
selves prais'd; and to an Eccho the pleasure of hearing your
selves talk.

WITWOUD.   But I know a Lady that loves talking so incessantly,   400
she won't give an Eccho fair play; she has that everlasting Rota-
tion of Tongue, that an Eccho must wait till she dies, before it can
catch her last Words.

MILLAMANT.   O Fiction; *Fainall*, let us leave these Men.

MIRABELL.   Draw off *Witwoud*.

Aside to MRS FAINALL.   405

MRS FAINALL.   Immediately; I have a Word or two for Mr
Witwoud.

MIRABELL.   I wou'd beg a little private Audience too——

Exit WITWOUD *and* MRS FAINALL.

You had the Tyranny to deny me last Night; tho' you knew I
came to impart a Secret to you, that concern'd my Love.   410

MILLAMANT.   You saw I was engag'd.

MIRABELL.   Unkind. You had the leisure to entertain a Herd of
Fools; Things who visit you from their excessive Idleness;
bestowing on your easiness that time, which is the incumbrance of
their Lives. How can you find delight in such Society? It is   415
impossible they should admire you, they are not capable: Or if
they were, it shou'd be to you as a Mortification; for sure to please
a Fool is some degree of Folly.

MILLAMANT.   I please my self——Besides sometimes to converse
with Fools, is for my Health.   420

MIRABELL.   Your Health! Is there a worse Disease than the
Conversation of Fools?

MILLAMANT.   Yes, the Vapours; Fools are Physick for it, next
to *Assa-fœtida*.

MIRABELL.   You are not in a Course of Fools?   425

MILLAMANT.   *Mirabell*, If you persist in this offensive Freedom
——You'll displease me——I think I must resolve after all, not
to have you——We shan't agree.

MIRABELL.   Not in our Physick it may be.

MILLAMANT.   And yet our Distemper in all likelihood will be the   430
same; for we shall be sick of one another. I shan't endure to be
reprimanded, nor instructed; 'tis so dull to act always by
Advice, and so tedious to be told of ones Faults——I can't bear
it. Well, I won't have you *Mirabell*——I'm resolved——I think
——You may go——Ha, ha, ha. What wou'd you give, that   435
you cou'd help loving me?

MIRABELL.   I would give something that you did not know, I
cou'd not help it.

MILLAMANT.   Come, don't look grave then. Well, what do you
say to me?   440

MIRABELL.   I say that a Man may as soon make a Friend by his
Wit, or a Fortune by his Honesty, as win a Woman with plain
Dealing and Sincerity.

MILLAMANT.   Sententious *Mirabell*! Prithee don't look with that
violent and inflexible wise Face, like *Solomon* at the dividing of the   445
Child in an old Tapestry-hanging.

MIRABELL.   You are merry, Madam, but I wou'd perswade you
for one Moment to be serious.

MILLAMANT.   What, with that Face? No, if you keep your Countenance, 'tis impossible I shou'd hold mine. Well, after all, there   450
is something very moving in a love-sick Face. Ha, ha, ha——
Well I won't laugh, don't be peevish——Heigho! Now I'll be
melancholly, as melancholly as a Watch-light. Well *Mirabell*, If
ever you will win me woo me now——Nay, if you are so tedious,
fare you well;——I see they are walking away.   455

MIRABELL.   Can you not find in the variety of your Disposition
one Moment——

MILLAMANT.   To hear you tell me that *Foible*'s married, and
your Plot like to speed——No.

MIRABELL.   But how you came to know it——   460

MILLAMANT.   Unless by the help of the Devil you can't imagine;
unless she shou'd tell me her self. Which of the two it may have
been, I will leave you to consider; and when you have done
thinking of that, think of me.

Exit.

MIRABELL.   I have something more——Gone——Think of you!   465
To think of a Whirlwind, tho' 'twere in a Whirlwind, were
a Case of more steady Contemplation; a very tranquility of Mind
and Mansion. A Fellow that lives in a Windmill, has not a more
whimsical Dwelling than the Heart of a Man that is lodg'd in a
Woman. There is no Point of the Compass to which they cannot   470
turn, and by which they are not turn'd; and by one as well as
another; for Motion not Method is their Occupation. To know
this, and yet continue to be in Love, is to be made wise from the
Dictates of Reason, and yet persevere to play the Fool by the
force of Instinct——O here come my pair of Turtles——What,   475
billing so sweetly! Is not *Valentine*'s Day over with you yet?

Enter WAITWELL *and* FOIBLE.

Sirrah, *Waitwell*, why sure you think you were married for your
own Recreation, and not for my Conveniency.

WAITWELL.   Your Pardon, Sir. With Submission, we have
indeed been solacing in lawful Delights; but still with an Eye to   480
Business, Sir. I have instructed her as well as I cou'd. If she can

take your Directions as readily as my Instructions, Sir, your
Affairs are in a prosperous way.

MIRABELL.   Give you Joy, Mrs. *Foible*.

FOIBLE.   O las Sir, I'm so asham'd——I'm afraid my Lady has   485
been in a thousand Inquietudes for me. But I protest, Sir, I made
much haste as I could.

WAITWELL.   That she did indeed, Sir. It was my Fault that she
did not make more.

MIRABELL.   That I believe.   490

FOIBLE.   But I told my Lady as you instructed me, Sir. That I had
a prospect of seeing Sir *Rowland* your Uncle; and that I wou'd
put her Ladyship's Picture in my Pocket to shew him; which I'll
be sure to say has made him so enamour'd of her Beauty, that he
burns with Impatience to lie at her Ladyship's Feet and worship   495
the Original.

MIRABELL.   Excellent *Foible*! Matrimony had made you eloquent
in Love.

WAITWELL.   I think she has profited, Sir. I think so.

FOIBLE.   You have seen Madam *Millamant*, Sir?   500

MIRABELL.   Yes.

FOIBLE.   I told her Sir, because I did not know that you might
find an Opportunity; she had so much Company last Night.

MIRABELL.   Your Diligence will merit more——In the mean
time——   505

Gives Mony.

FOIBLE.   O dear Sir, your humble Servant.

WAITWELL.   Spouse.

MIRABELL.   Stand off Sir, not a Penny——Go on and prosper,
Foible——The Lease shall be made good and the Farm stock'd,
if we succeed.   510

FOIBLE.   I don't question your Generosity, Sir: And you need
not doubt of Success. If you have no more Commands Sir, I'll
gone; I'm sure my Lady is at her Toilet, and can't dress till I
come——O Dear, I'm sure that was Mrs. *Marwood* that went by

Looking out.

in a Mask; if she has seen me with you I'm sure she'll tell my Lady.   515
I'll make haste home and prevent her. Your Servant Sir. B'w'y
Waitwell.

Exit FOIBLE.

WAITWELL.   Sir *Rowland* if you please. The Jade's so pert upon her Preferment she forgets her self.

MIRABELL.   Come Sir, will you endeavour to forget your self ——And transform into Sir *Rowland*.   520

WAITWELL.   Why Sir; it will be impossible I shou'd remember my self——Married, Knighted and attended all in one Day! 'Tis enough to make any Man forget himself. The Difficulty will be how to recover my Acquaintance and Familiarity with my   525 former self; and fall from my Transformation to a Reformation into *Waitwell*. Nay, I shan't be quite the same *Waitwell* neither ——For now I remember me, I am married, and can't be my own Man again.

> Ay there's the Grief; that's the sad change of Life;   530
> To lose my Title, and yet keep my Wife.

Exeunt.

ACT III

SCENE I

A Room in Lady Wishfort's House

LADY WISHFORT *at her Toilet*, PEG *waiting*.

LADY WISHFORT.   Merciful, no News of *Foible* yet?

PEG.   No, Madam.

LADY WISHFORT.   I have no more patience——If I have not fretted my self till I am pale again, there's no Veracity in me. Fetch me the Red——The Red, do you hear, Sweet-heart? An   5 errant Ash colour, as I'm a Person. Look you how this Wench stirs! Why dost thou not fetch me a little Red? Did'st thou not hear me, Mopus?

PEG.   The red *Ratifia* does your Ladyship mean, or the Cherry Brandy?   10

LADY WISHFORT.   *Ratifia*, Fool. No Fool. Not the *Ratifia* Fool——Grant me patience! I mean the *Spanish* Paper Idiot, Complexion Darling. Paint, Paint, Paint, dost thou understand that, Changeling, dangling thy Hands like Bobbins before thee. Why dost thou not stir Puppet? thou wooden Thing upon Wires.　　15

PEG. Lord, Madam, your Ladyship is so impatient——I cannot come at the Paint, Madam; Mrs. *Foible* has lock'd it up, and carry'd the Key with her.

LADY WISHFORT. A Pox take you both——Fetch me the Cherry-Brandy then——　　20

Exit PEG.

I'm as pale and as faint, I look like Mrs. Qualmsick the Curate's Wife, that's always breeding——Wench, come, come, Wench, what art thou doing, Sipping? Tasting? Save thee, dost thou not know the Bottle?　　25

Enter PEG *with a Bottle and China-cup.*

PEG. Madam, I was looking for a Cup.

LADY WISHFORT. A Cup, save thee, and what a Cup hast thou brought! Dost thou take me for a *Fairy*, to drink out of an *Acorn*? Why didst thou not bring thy Thimble? Hast thou ne'er a Brass-Thimble clinking in thy Pocket with a bit of Nutmeg? I warrant thee. Come, fill, fill.——So——again. See who that is——　　30

One knocks.

Set down the Bottle first. Here, here, under the Table—— What, wou'dst thou go with the Bottle in thy Hand like a Tapster. As I'm a Person, this Wench has liv'd in an Inn upon the Road, before she came to me, like *Maritornes* the *Asturian* in *Don Quixote*. No *Foible* yet?　　35

PEG. No Madam, Mrs. *Marwood*.

LADY WISHFORT. O *Marwood*, let her come in. Come in good *Marwood*.

Enter MRS MARWOOD.

MRS MARWOOD. I'm surpriz'd to find your Ladyship in *dishabilie* at this time of day.　　40

LADY WISHFORT. *Foible*'s a lost Thing; has been abroad since Morning, and never heard of since.

MRS MARWOOD.   I saw her but now, as I came mask'd through
the Park, in Conference with *Mirabell*.   45

LADY WISHFORT.   With *Mirabell*! You call my Blood into my
Face, with mentioning that Traytor. She durst not have the
Confidence. I sent her to Negotiate an Affair, in which if I'm
detected I'm undone. If that wheadling Villain has wrought upon
Foible to detect me, I'm ruin'd. Oh my dear Friend, I'm a Wretch   50
of Wretches if I'm detected.

MRS MARWOOD.   O Madam, you cannot suspect Mrs. *Foible*'s
Integrity.

LADY WISHFORT.   O, he carries Poyson in his Tongue that
wou'd corrupt Integrity it self. If she has given him an Oppor-   55
tunity, she has as good as put her Integrity into his Hands. Ah
dear *Marwood*, what's Integrity to an Opportunity?——Hark!
I hear her——Go you Thing and send her in.

Exit PEG.

Dear Friend retire into my Closet, that I may examine her with
more freedom——You'll pardon me dear Friend, I can make bold   60
with you——There are Books over the Chimney——
Quarles and *Pryn*, and the *Short View of the Stage*, with *Bunyan*'s
Works to entertain you.

Exit MRS MARWOOD.

Enter FOIBLE.

O *Foible*, where has thou been? What hast thou been doing?

FOIBLE.   Madam, I have seen the Party.   65

LADY WISHFORT.   But what hast thou done?

FOIBLE.   Nay, 'tis your Ladyship has done, and are to do; I have
only promis'd. But a Man so enamour'd——So transported!
Well, here it is, all that is left; all that is not kiss'd away——
Well, if worshipping of Pictures be a Sin——Poor Sir *Rowland*,   70
I say.

LADY WISHFORT.   The Miniature has been counted like——
But hast thou not betray'd me, *Foible*? Hast thou not detected
me to that faithless *Mirabell*?——What had'st thou to do with
him in the Park? Answer me, has he got nothing out of thee?   75

FOIBLE.   So, the Devil has been before-hand with me, what shall
I say?——Alas, Madam, cou'd I help it, if I met that confident

Thing? Was I in Fault? If you had heard how he us'd me, and all upon your Ladyship's Account, I'm sure you wou'd not suspect my Fidelity. Nay, if that had been the worst I cou'd have born: But he had a Fling at your Ladyship too; and then I could not hold; But Ifaith I gave him his own.

LADY WISHFORT.   Me? What did the filthy Fellow say?

FOIBLE.   O Madam; 'tis a shame to say what he said—— With his Taunts and his Fleers, tossing up his Nose. Humh (says he) what you are a hatching some Plot (says he) you are so early abroad, or Catering (says he) ferreting for some disbanded Officer I warrant——Half Pay is but thin Subsistance (says he) ——Well, what Pension does your Lady propose? Let me see (says he) what she must come down pretty deep now, she's super-annuated (says he) and——

LADY WISHFORT.   Ods my Life, I'll have him, I'll have him murder'd. I'll have him poyson'd. Where does he eat? I'll marry a Drawer to have him poyson'd in his Wine. I'll send for *Robin* from *Lockets*——Immediately.

FOIBLE.   Poyson him? Poysoning's too good for him. Starve him Madam, starve him, marry Sir *Rowland* and get him disinherited. O you would bless your self, to hear what he said.

LADY WISHFORT.   A Villain, superanuated!

FOIBLE.   Humh (says he) I hear you are laying Designs against me too (says he), and Mrs. *Millamant* is to marry my Uncle; (he does not suspect a Word of your Ladyship;) but (says he) I'll fit you for that, I warrant you (says he) I'll hamper you for that (says he) you and your old Frippery too (says he) I'll handle you——

LADY WISHFORT.   Audacious Villain! handle me, wou'd he durst——Frippery? old Frippery! Was there ever such a foul-mouth'd Fellow? I'll be married to Morrow, I'll be contracted to Night.

FOIBLE.   The sooner the better, Madam.

LADY WISHFORT.   Will Sir *Rowland* be here, say'st thou? when *Foible*?

FOIBLE.   Incontinently, Madam. No new Sheriff's Wife expects the return of her Husband after Knighthood, with that Impatience in which Sir *Rowland* burns for the dear hour of kissing your Ladyship's Hands after Dinner.

LADY WISHFORT. Frippery? Superannuated Frippery! I'll Frippery the Villain; I'll reduce him to Frippery and Rags. A Tatterdemallion——I hope to see him hung with Tatters, like a Long-Lane Pent-house, or a Gibbet-thief. A slander-mouth'd 120 Railer: I warrant the Spendthrift Prodigal's in Debt as much as the Million Lottery, or the whole Court upon a Birth day. I'll spoil his Credit with his Taylor. Yes, he shall have my Niece with her Fortune, he shall.

FOIBLE.   He! I hope to see him lodge in *Ludgate* first, and Angle 125 into *Black Friers* for Brass Farthings, with an old Mitten.

LADY WISHFORT.   Ay dear *Foible*; thank thee for that dear *Foible*. He has put me out of all patience. I shall never recompose my Features, to receive Sir *Rowland* with any Oeconomy of Face. This Wretch has fretted me that I am absolutely decay'd. Look 130 *Foible*.

FOIBLE.   Your Ladyship has frown'd a little rashly, indeed Madam. There are some Cracks discernable in the white Vernish.

LADY WISHFORT.   Let me see the Glass——Cracks, say'st thou? Why I am arrantly flea'd——I look like an old peel'd 135 Wall. Thou must repair me *Foible*, before Sir *Rowland* comes; or I shall never keep up to my Picture.

FOIBLE.   I warrant you, Madam; a little Art once made your Picture like you; and now a little of the same Art, must make you like your Picture. Your Picture must sit for you, Madam. 140

LADY WISHFORT.   But art thou sure Sir *Rowland* will not fail to come? Or will a not fail when he does come? Will he be Importunate *Foible*, and push? For if he shou'd not be Importunate——I shall never break Decorums——I shall die with Confusion, if I am forc'd to advance——Oh no, I can never 145 advance——I shall swoon if he shou'd expect advances. No, I hope Sir *Rowland* is better bred, than to put a Lady to the necessity of breaking her Forms. I won't be too coy neither.——I won't give him despair——But a little Disdain is not amiss; a little Scorn is alluring. 150

FOIBLE.   A little Scorn becomes your Ladyship.

LADY WISHFORT.   Yes, but Tenderness becomes me best—— A sort of a dyingness——You see that Picture has a sort of a—— Ha *Foible*? A swimminess in the Eyes——Yes, I'll look so—— My Niece affects it; but she wants Features. Is Sir *Rowland* 155

handsome? Let my Toilet be remov'd——I'll dress above. I'll
receive Sir *Rowland* here. Is he handsome? Don't answer me. I
won't know: I'll be surpriz'd. I'll be taken by Surprize.

FOIBLE.   By Storm, Madam. Sir *Rowland*'s a brisk Man.

LADY WISHFORT.   Is he! O then he'll Importune, if he's a   160
brisk Man. I shall save Decorums if Sir *Rowland* importunes. I
have a mortal Terror at the apprehension of offending against
Decorums. Nothing but Importunity can surmount Decorums.
O I'm glad he's a brisk Man. Let my Things be remov'd, good
Foible.   165

                                                               Exit.

Enter MRS FAINALL.

MRS FAINALL.   O *Foible*, I have been in a Fright least I shou'd
come too late. That Devil *Marwood* saw you in the Park with
Mirabell, and I'm afraid will discover it to my Lady.

FOIBLE.   Discover what, Madam?

MRS FAINALL.   Nay, nay, put not on that strange Face. I am   170
privy to the whole Design, and know that *Waitwell*, to whom
thou wert this morning Married, is to personate *Mirabell*'s Uncle,
and as such winning my Lady, to involve her in those Difficulties,
from which *Mirabell* only must release her, by his making his
Conditions to have my Cousin and her Fortune left to her own   175
disposal.

FOIBLE.   O dear Madam, I beg your Pardon. It was not my
Confidence in your Ladyship that was deficient; but I thought
the former good Correspondence between your Ladyship
and Mr. *Mirabell* might have hinder'd his communicating this
Secret.   180

MRS FAINALL.   Dear *Foible* forget that.

FOIBLE.   O dear Madam, Mr. *Mirabell* is such a sweet winning
Gentleman——But your Ladyship is the Pattern of Generosity.
——Sweet Lady, to be so good! Mr. *Mirabell* cannot chuse but
be grateful. I find your Ladyship has his Heart still. Now, Madam,   185
I can safely tell your Ladyship our success, Mrs. *Marwood* had told
my Lady; but I warrant I manag'd my self. I turn'd it all for the
better. I told my Lady that Mr. *Mirabell* rail'd at her. I laid horrid
Things to his charge, I'll vow; and my Lady is so incens'd, that
she'll be contracted to Sir *Rowland* to Night, she says;——I   190

warrant I work'd her up, that he may have her for asking for, as
they say of a *Welch* Maiden-head.

MRS FAINALL.   O rare *Foible*!

FOIBLE.   Madam, I beg your Ladyship to acquaint Mr. *Mirabell*
of his success. I wou'd be seen as little as possible to speak to   195
him,——besides, I believe Madam *Marwood* watches me.——
She has a Month's mind; but I know Mr. *Mirabell* can't abide
her.——

Enter FOOTMAN.

John——remove my Lady's Toilet. Madam your Servant.
My Lady is so impatient, I fear she'll come for me, if I stay.   200

MRS FAINALL.   I'll go with you up the back Stairs, lest I shou'd
meet her.

Exeunt.

Enter MRS MARWOOD.

MRS MARWOOD.   Indeed Mrs. Engine, is it thus with you? Are
you become a go-between of this Importance? Yes, I shall watch
you. Why this Wench is the *Pass-par-tout*, a very Master-Key to   205
every Bodies strong Box. My Friend *Fainall*, have you carried it
so swimmingly? I thought there was something in it; but it seems
it's over with you. Your loathing is not from a want of Appetite
then, but from a Surfeit. Else you could never be so cool to fall
from a Principal to be an Assistant; to procure for him! A   210
Pattern of Generosity, that I confess. Well, Mr. *Fainall*, you have
met with your Match.——O Man, Man! Woman, Woman! The
Devil's an Ass: If I were a Painter, I wou'd draw him like an Idiot,
a Driveler, with a Bib and Bells. Man shou'd have his Head and
Horns, and Woman the rest of him. Poor simple Fiend! Madam   215
Marwood has a Months Mind, but he can't abide her——'Twere
better for him you had not been his Confessor in that Affair;
without you cou'd have kept his Counsel closer. I shall not
prove another Pattern of Generosity; and stalk for him, till he
takes his Stand to aim at a Fortune, he has not oblig'd me to that,   220
with those Excesses of himself; and now I'll have none of him.
Here comes the good Lady, panting ripe; with a Heart full of
Hope, and a Head full of Care, like any Chymist upon the Day of
Projection.

Enter LADY WISHFORT.

LADY WISHFORT.   O dear *Marwood* what shall I say, for this   225
rude forgetfulness——But my dear Friend is all Goodness.

MRS MARWOOD.   No Apologies, dear Madam. I have been very
well entertained.

LADY WISHFORT.   As I'm a Person I am in a very Chaos to
think I shou'd so forget my self——But I have such an Olio of   230
Affairs really I know not what to do——[*Calls.*]——*Foible*——
I expect my Nephew Sir *Wilfull* every moment too——Why
Foible——He means to Travel for Improvement.

MRS MARWOOD.   Methinks Sir *Wilfull* should rather think of
Marrying than Travelling at his Years. I hear he is turn'd of   235
Forty.

LADY WISHFORT.   O he's in less Danger of being spoil'd by
his Travels——I am against my Nephews marrying too young.
It will be time enough when he comes back, and has acquir'd
Discretion to choose for himself.   240

MRS MARWOOD.   Methinks Mrs. *Millamant* and he wou'd make
a very fit Match. He may Travel afterwards. 'Tis a Thing very
usual with young Gentlemen.

LADY WISHFORT.   I promise you I have thought on't——And
since 'tis your Judgment, I'll think on't again. I assure you I will;   245
I value your Judgment extreamly. On my Word I'll propose it.

Enter FOIBLE.

Come, come *Foible*——I had forgot my Nephew will be
here before Dinner——I must make haste.

FOIBLE.   Mr. *Witwoud* and Mr. *Petulant*, are come to Dine with
your Ladyship.   250

LADY WISHFORT.   O Dear, I can't appear till I'm dress'd.
Dear *Marwood* shall I be free with you again, and beg you to
entertain 'em. I'll make all imaginable haste. Dear Friend excuse
me.

Exit LADY WISHFORT *and* FOIBLE.

Enter MILLAMANT *and* MINCING.

MILLAMANT.   Sure never any thing was so Unbred as that   255
odious Man——*Marwood*, your Servant.

MRS MARWOOD.   You have a Colour, what's the matter?

MILLAMANT.   That horrid Fellow *Petulant*, has provok'd me
into a Flame——I have broke my Fan——*Mincing*, lend me
yours;——Is not all the Powder out of my Hair?   260

MRS MARWOOD.   No. What has he done?

MILLAMANT.   Nay, he has done nothing; he has only talk'd——
Nay, he has said nothing neither; but he has contradicted every
Thing that has been said. For my part, I thought *Witwoud* and
he wou'd have quarrell'd.   265

MINCING.   I vow Mem, I thought once they wou'd have fit.

MILLAMANT.   Well, 'tis a lamentable thing I'll swear, that one
has not the liberty of choosing one's Acquaintance, as one does
one's Cloaths.

MRS MARWOOD.   If we had the liberty, we shou'd be as weary of   270
one Set of Acquaintance, tho' never so good, as we are of one
Suit, tho' never so fine. A Fool and a *Doily* Stuff wou'd now and
then find Days of Grace, and be worn for variety.

MILLAMANT.   I could consent to wear 'em, if they wou'd wear
alike; but Fools never wear out——they are such *Drap-du-berry* 275
Things! without one cou'd give 'em to one's Chambermaid after
a day or two.

MRS MARWOOD.   'Twere better so indeed. Or what think you
of the Play-house? A fine gay glossy Fool shou'd be given there,
like a new masking Habit, after the Masquerade is over, and we 280
have done with the Disguise. For a Fool's Visit is always a
Disguise; and never admitted by a Woman of Wit, but to blind
her Affair with a Lover of Sense. If you wou'd but appear
bare fac'd now, and own *Mirabell*; you might as easily
put off *Petulant* and *Witwoud*, as your Hood and Scarf. And   285
indeed 'tis time, for the Town has found it: The Secret is
grown too big for the Pretence: 'Tis like Mrs. *Primly*'s great
Belly; she may lace it down before, but it burnishes on her
Hips. Indeed, *Millamant*, you can no more conceal it, then
my Lady *Strammel* can her Face, that goodly Face, which in   290
defiance of her Rhenish-wine Tea, will not be comprehended
in a Mask.

MILLAMANT.   I'll take my Death, *Marwood*, you are more Censorious, than a decay'd Beauty, or a discarded Tost; *Mincing*, tell

the Men they may come up. My Aunt is not dressing; their Folly   295
is less provoking than your Mallice.

Exit MINCING.

The Town has found it. What has it found? That *Mirabell* loves
me is no more a Secret, than it is a Secret that you discover'd
it to my Aunt, or than the Reason why you discover'd it is a
Secret.   300

MRS MARWOOD.   You are nettl'd.

MILLAMANT.   You'r mistaken. Ridiculous!

MRS MARWOOD.   Indeed my Dear, you'll tear another Fan, if
you don't mitigate those violent Airs.

MILLAMANT.   O silly! Ha, ha, ha. I cou'd laugh immoderately.   305
Poor *Mirabell*! his Constancy to me has quite destroy'd his
Complaisance for all the World beside. I swear, I never enjoin'd
it him, to be so coy——If I had the Vanity to think he wou'd
obey me; I wou'd command him to shew more Gallantry——
'Tis hardly well bred to be so particular on one Hand, and so   310
insensible on the other. But I despair to prevail, and so let him
follow his own way. Ha, ha, ha, Pardon me, dear Creature, I
must laugh, Ha, ha, ha; tho' I grant you 'tis a little barbarous,
Ha, ha, ha.

MRS MARWOOD.   What pity 'tis, so much fine Raillery, and   315
deliver'd with so significant Gesture, shou'd be so unhappily
directed to miscarry.

MILLAMANT.   Hæ? Dear Creature I ask your Pardon——I
swear I did not mind you.

MRS MARWOOD.   Mr. *Mirabell* and you both, may think it a   320
Thing impossible, when I shall tell him, by telling you——

MILLAMANT.   O Dear, what? for it is the same thing, if I hear
it——Ha, ha, ha.

MRS MARWOOD.   That I detest him, hate him, Madam.

MILLAMANT.   O Madam, why so do I——And yet the Creature   325
loves me, Ha, ha, ha. How can one forbear laughing to think of
it——I am a Sybil if I am not amaz'd to think what he can see
in me. I'll take my Death, I think you are handsomer——And
within a Year or two as young.——If you cou'd but stay for me,
I shou'd overtake you——But that cannot be——Well, that   330
Thought makes me Melancholly——Now I'll be sad.

c

Mrs Marwood.   Your merry Note may be chang'd sooner than you think.

Millamant.   Dee say so? Then I'm resolv'd I'll have a Song to keep up my Spirits.   335

Enter Mincing.

Mincing.   The Gentlemen stay but to Comb, Madam; and will wait on you.

Millamant.   Desire Mrs. —— that is in the next Room to sing the Song, I wou'd have learnt Yesterday. You shall hear it Madam——Not that here's any great matter in it——But 'tis   340 agreeable to my Humour.

Set by Mr. John Eccles, *and sung by Mrs.* Hodgson.

SONG

I.

Love's but the frailty of the Mind,
When 'tis not with Ambition join'd;
A sickly Flame, which if not fed expires;
And feeding, wasts in Self-consuming Fires.   345

II.

'Tis not to wound a wanton Boy
Or am'rous Youth, that gives the Joy;
But 'tis the Glory to have pierc'd a Swain,
For whom inferiour Beauties sigh'd in vain.

III.

Then I alone the Conquest prize   350
When I insult a Rival's Eyes:
If there's Delight in Love, 'tis when I see
That Heart which others bleed for, bleed for me.

Enter Petulant *and* Witwoud.

Millamant.   Is your Animosity compos'd, Gentlemen?

WITWOUD. Raillery, Raillery, Madam, we have no Animosity 355
——We hit off a little Wit now and then, but no Animosity——
The falling out of Wits is like the falling out of Lovers——We
agree in the main, like Treble and Base. Ha, *Petulant*!

PETULANT. Ay in the main——But when I have a Humour to
contradict.   360

WITWOUD. Ay, when he has a Humour to contradict, then I
contradict too. What, I know my Cue. Then we contradict one
another like two Battle-dores: For Contradictions beget one
another like *Jews*.

PETULANT. If he says Black's Black——If I have a Humour to 365
say 'tis Blue——Let that pass——All's one for that. If I have a
Humour to prove it, it must be granted.

WITWOUD. Not positively must——But it may——It may.

PETULANT. Yes, it positively must, upon Proof positive.

WITWOUD. Ay, upon Proof positive it must; but upon Proof 370
presumptive it only may. That's a Logical Distinction now,
Madam.

MRS MARWOOD. I perceive your Debates are of Importance and
very learnedly handl'd.

PETULANT. Importance is one Thing, and Learning's another; 375
but a Debate's a Debate, that I assert.

WITWOUD. *Petulant*'s an Enemy to Learning; he relies altogether
on his Parts.

PETULANT. No, I'm no Enemy to Learning; it hurts not me.

MRS MARWOOD. That's a Sign indeed its no Enemy to you. 380

PETULANT. No, no, it's no Enemy to any Body, but them that
have it.

MILLAMANT. Well, an illiterate Man's my Aversion. I wonder
at the Impudence of any Illiterate Man, to offer to make Love.

WITWOUD. That I confess I wonder at too.   385

MILLAMANT. Ah! to marry an Ignorant! that can hardly Read
or Write.

PETULANT. Why shou'd a Man be ever the further from being
married tho' he can't Read, any more than he is from being
Hang'd. The Ordinary's paid for setting the *Psalm*, and the 390
Parish-Priest for reading the Ceremony. And for the rest which
is to follow in both Cases, a Man may do it without Book——
So all's one for that.

MILLAMANT.   Dee hear the Creature? Lord, here's Company, I'll be gone.

395

Exeunt MILLAMANT *and* MINCING.

WITWOUD.   In the Name of *Bartlemew* and his Fair, what have we here?

MRS MARWOOD.   'Tis your Brother, I fancy, Don't you know him?

WITWOUD.   Not I——Yes, I think it is he——I've almost forgot him; I have not seen him since the Revolution.

Enter SIR WILFULL WITWOUD *in a Country Riding Habit, and* SERVANT *to* LADY WISHFORT.

SERVANT.   Sir, my Lady's dressing. Here's Company; if you please to walk in, in the mean time.

SIR WILFULL.   Dressing! What it's but Morning here I warrant with you in *London*; we shou'd count it towards Afternoon in our Parts, down in *Shropshire*——Why then belike my Aunt han't din'd yet——Ha, Friend?

405

SERVANT.   Your Aunt, Sir?

SIR WILFULL.   My Aunt Sir, yes my Aunt Sir, and your Lady Sir; your Lady is my Aunt, Sir——Why, what do'st thou not know me, Friend? Why then send Somebody here that does. How long hast thou liv'd with thy Lady, Fellow, ha!

410

SERVANT.   A Week, Sir; longer than any Body in the House, except my Lady's Woman.

SIR WILFULL.   Why then belike thou dost not know thy Lady, thou see'st her, ha Friend?

415

SERVANT.   Why truly Sir, I cannot safely swear to her Face in a Morning, before she is dress'd. 'Tis like I may give a shrew'd guess at her by this time.

SIR WILFULL.   Well prithee try what thou can'st do; if thou can'st not guess, enquire her out, do'st hear Fellow? And tell her, her Nephew Sir *Wilfull Witwoud* is in the House.

420

SERVANT.   I shall, Sir.

SIR WILFULL.   Hold ye, hear me Friend; a Word with you in your Ear, prithee who are these Gallants?

425

SERVANT.   Really Sir, I can't tell; here come so many here, 'tis hard to know 'em all.

Exit SERVANT.

Sir Wilfull.   Oons this Fellow knows less than a Starling;
I don't think a' knows his own Name.

Mrs Marwood.   Mr. *Witwoud*, your Brother is not behind Hand   430
in forgetfulness—I fancy he has forgot you too.

Witwoud.   I hope so——The Devil take him that remembers
first, I say.

Sir Wilfull.   Save you Gentlemen and Lady.

Mrs Marwood.   For shame Mr. *Witwoud*; why won't you speak   435
to him?——And you, Sir.

Witwoud.   *Petulant* speak.

Petulant.   And you, Sir.

Sir Wilfull.   No Offence, I hope.

Salutes Mrs Marwood.

Mrs Marwood. No sure, Sir.   440

Witwoud.   This is a vile Dog, I see that already. No Offence!
Ha, ha, ha, to him; to him *Petulant*, smoke him.

Petulant.   It seems as if you had come a Journey, Sir; hem,
hem.

Surveying him round.

Sir Wilfull.   Very likely, Sir, that it may seem so.   445

Petulant.   No Offence, I hope, Sir.

Witwoud.   Smoke the Boots, the Boots; *Petulant*, the Boots;
Ha, ha, ha.

Sir Wilful.   May be not, Sir; thereafter as 'tis meant, Sir.

Petulant.   Sir, I presume upon the Information of your   450
Boots.

Sir Wilfull.   Why, 'tis like you may, Sir: If you are not
satisfy'd with the Information of my Boots, Sir, if you will step
to the Stable, you may enquire further of my Horse, Sir.

Petulant.   Your Horse, Sir! Your Horse is an Ass, Sir!

Sir Wilfull.   Do you speak by way of Offence, Sir?   455

Mrs Marwood.   The Gentleman's merry, that's all, Sir——
S'life, we shall have a Quarrel betwixt an Horse and an Ass, before
they find one another out. You must not take any Thing amiss
from your Friends, Sir. You are among your Friends here, tho'
it may be you don't know it——If I am not mistaken, you are   460
Sir *Willfull Witwoud*.

Sir Wilfull.   Right Lady; I am Sir *Willfull Witwoud*, so I

write my self; no offence to any Body, I hope; and Nephew to the
Lady *Wishfort*, of this Mansion.

MRS MARWOOD.   Don't you know this Gentleman, Sir?   465

SIR WILFULL.   Hum! What sure 'tis not——Yea by'r Lady,
but 'tis——'Sheart I know not whether 'tis or no——Yea but
'tis, by the Rekin. Brother *Anthony*! What *Tony* Ifaith! What
do'st thou not know me? By'r Lady nor I thee, thou art so
Becravated, and Beperriwig'd——'Sheart why do'st not speak?   470
Art thou o'er-joy'd?

WITWOUD.   Odso Brother, is it you? Your Servant Brother.

SIR WILFULL.   Your Servant! Why yours, Sir. Your Servant
again——'Sheart, and your Friend and Servant to that——And
a——[*puff*]and a flap Dragon for your Service, Sir: And a Hare's   475
Foot, and a Hare's Scut for your Service, Sir; an you be so cold
and so courtly!

WITWOUD.   No offence, I hope, Brother.

SIR WILFULL.   'Sheart, Sir, but there is, and much offence.——
A pox, is this your Inns o' Court breeding, not to know your   480
Friends and your Relations, your Elders, and your Betters?

WITWOUD.   Why Brother *Willfull* of *Salop*, you may be as short
as a *Shrewsbury* Cake, if you please. But I tell you, 'tis not modish
to know Relations in Town. You think you're in the Country,
where great lubberly Brothers slabber and kiss one another when   485
they meet, like a Call of Serjeants——'Tis not the fashion here;
'tis not indeed, dear Brother.

SIR WILFULL.   The Fashion's a Fool; and you're a Fop, dear
Brother. 'Sheart, I've suspected this——By'r Lady I conjectur'd
you were a Fop, since you began to change the Stile of your   490
Letters, and write in a scrap of Paper gilt round the Edges, no
broader than a *Subpœna*. I might expect this, when you left off
Honour'd Brother; and hoping you are in good Health, and so
forth——To begin with a Rat me, Knight, I'm so sick of a last
Nights debauch——O'ds heart, and then tell a familiar Tale of a   495
Cock and a Bull, and a Whore and a Bottle, and so conclude——
You cou'd write News before you were out of your Time, when
you liv'd with honest *Pumple Nose* the Attorney of *Furnival*'s Inn
——You cou'd intreat to be remember'd then to your Friends
round the *Rekin*. We cou'd have Gazetts then, and *Dawks*'s Letter,   500
and the weekly Bill, 'till of late Days.

PETULANT.   S'life, *Witwoud*, were you ever an Attorney's Clerk? Of the Family of the *Furnivals*. Ha, ha, ha!

WITWOUD.   Ay, ay, but that was for a while. Not long, not long; pshaw, I was not in my own Power then. An Orphan, and this Fellow was my Guardian; ay, ay, I was glad to consent to that, Man, to come to *London*. He had the disposal of me then. If I had not agreed to that, I might have been bound Prentice to a Felt-maker in *Shrewsbury*; this Fellow wou'd have bound me to a Maker of Felts.

SIR WILFULL.   'Sheart, and better than to be bound to a Maker of Fops; where, I suppose, you have serv'd your Time; and now you may set up for your self.

MRS MARWOOD.   You intend to Travel, Sir, as I'm inform'd.

SIR WILFULL.   Belike I may Madam. I may chance to sail upon the salt Seas, if my Mind hold.

PETULANT.   And the Wind serve.

SIR WILFULL.   Serve or not serve, I shant ask License of you, Sir; nor the Weather-Cock your Companion. I direct my Discourse to the Lady, Sir: 'Tis like my Aunt may have told you, Madam——Yes, I have settl'd my Concerns, I may say now, and am minded to see Foreign Parts. If an how that the Peace holds, whereby that is, Taxes abate.

MRS MARWOOD.   I thought you had design'd for *France* at all Adventures.

SIR WILFULL.   I can't tell that; 'tis like I may, and 'tis like I may not. I am somewhat dainty in making a Resolution,——because when I make it I keep it. I don't stand shill I, shall I, then; if I say't, I'll do't: But I have Thoughts to tarry a small matter in Town, to learn somewhat of your *Lingo* first, before I cross the Seas. I'd gladly have a spice of your *French* as they say, whereby to hold discourse in Foreign Countries.

MRS MARWOOD.   Here is an Academy in Town for that use.

SIR WILFULL.   There is? 'Tis like there may.

MRS MARWOOD.   No doubt you will return very much improv'd.

WITWOUD.   Yes, refin'd, like a *Dutch* Skipper from a Whale-fishing.

Enter LADY WISHFORT *and* FAINALL.

LADY WISHFORT.   Nephew, you are welcome.

SIR WILFULL.   Aunt, your Servant.   540

FAINALL.   Sir *Willfull*, your most faithful Servant.

SIR WILFULL.   Cousin *Fainall*, give me your Hand.

LADY WISHFORT.   Cousin *Witwoud*, your Servant; Mr. *Petulant*, your Servant.——Nephew, you are welcome again. Will you drink any Thing after your Journey, Nephew, before   545 you eat? Dinner's almost ready.

SIR WILFULL.   I'm very well I thank you Aunt——However, I thank you for your courteous Offer. 'Sheart, I was afraid you wou'd have been in the fashion too, and have remember'd to have forgot your Relations. Here's your Cousin *Tony*, belike, I may'nt   550 call him Brother for fear of offence.

LADY WISHFORT.   O he's a Rallier, Nephew——My Cousin's a Wit. And your great Wits always rally their best Friends to chuse. When you have been abroad, Nephew, you'll understand Raillery better.   555

FAINALL and MRS MARWOOD talk apart.

SIR WILFULL.   Why then let him hold his Tongue in the mean time; and rail when that day comes.

Enter MINCING.

MINCING.   Mem, I come to acquaint your Laship that Dinner is impatient.

SIR WILFULL.   Impatient? Why then belike it won't stay, 'till   560 I pull off my Boots. Sweet-heart, can you help me to a pair of Slippers?——My Man's with his Horses, I warrant.

LADY WISHFORT.   Fie, fie, Nephew, you wou'd not pull off your Boots here——Go down into the Hall——Dinner shall stay for you——My Nephew's a little unbred, you'll pardon   565 him, Madam——Gentlemen will you walk? *Marwood*?

MRS MARWOOD.   I'll follow you, Madam——Before Sir *Willfull* is ready.

Manent MRS MARWOOD and FAINALL.

FAINALL.   Why then *Foible*'s a Bawd, an Errant, Rank, Match-making Bawd. And I it seems am a Husband, a Rank-Husband;   570 and my Wife a very Errant, Rank-Wife,——all in the Way of the

World. 'S death to be an Anticipated Cuckold, a Cuckold in Embrio? Sure I was born with budding Antlers like a young Satyre, or a Citizens Child. 'S death to be Out-Witted, to be Out-Jilted——Out-Matrimony'd,——If I had kept my speed *575* like a Stag, 'twere somewhat,——but to crawl after, with my Horns like a Snail, and out-strip'd by my Wife——'tis Scurvy Wedlock.

MRS MARWOOD. Then shake it off, You have often wish'd for an opportunity to part;——and now you have it. But first *580* prevent their Plot,——the half of *Millamant*'s Fortune is too Considerable to be parted with, to a Foe, to *Mirabell*.

FAINALL. Dam him, that had been mine——had you not made that fond discovery——that had been forfeited, had they been Married. My Wife had added Lustre to my Horns, by that *585* Encrease of fortune,——I cou'd have worn 'em tipt with Gold, tho' my forehead had been furnish'd like a Deputy-Lieutenant's Hall.

MRS MARWOOD. They may prove a Cap of Maintenance to you still, if you can away with your Wife. And she's no worse than *590* when you had her——I dare swear she had given up her Game, before she was Marry'd.

FAINALL. Hum! That may be——She might throw up her Cards; but Ile be hang'd if she did not put Pam in her Pocket.

MRS MARWOOD. You Married her to keep you; and if you can *595* contrive to have her keep you better than you expected; why should you not keep her longer than you intended?

FAINALL. The means, the means.

MRS MARWOOD. Discover to my Lady your Wife's conduct; threaten to part with her——My Lady loves her, and will come *600* to any Composition to save her reputation, take the opportunity of breaking it, just upon the discovery of this imposture. My Lady will be enraged beyond bounds, and Sacrifice Neice, and Fortune, and all at that Conjuncture. And let me alone to keep her warm, if she should Flag in her part, I will not fail to prompt *605* her.

FAINALL. Faith this has an appearance.

MRS MARWOOD. I'm sorry I hinted to my Lady to endeavour a match between *Millamant* and Sir *Wilfull*, that may be an Obstacle.

610

FAINALL.   O, for that matter leave me to manage him; I'll disable him for that, he will drink like a *Dane*: after dinner, I'll set his hand in.

MRS MARWOOD.   Well, how do you stand affected towards your Lady?   615

FAINALL.   Why faith I'm thinking of it.——Let me see——I am married already; so that's over,——my Wife has plaid the Jade with me——Well, that's over too——I never lov'd her, or if I had, why that wou'd have been over too by this time——Jealous of her I cannot be, for I am certain; so there's an end of Jealousie.   620 Weary of her, I am, and shall be——No, there's no end of that; No, no, that were too much to hope. Thus far concerning my repose. Now for my Reputation,——As to my own, I married not for it; so that's out of the Question,——And as to my part in my Wife's——Why she had parted with hers before; so bring-   625 ing none to me, she can take none from me, 'tis against all rule of Play, that I should lose to one, who has not wherewithal to stake.

MRS MARWOOD.   Besides you forget, Marriage is honourable.

FAINALL.   Hum! Faith and that's well thought on; Marriage is   630 honourable as you say; and if so, Wherefore should Cuckoldom be a discredit, being deriv'd from so honourable a root?

MRS MARWOOD.   Nay I know not; if the root be Honourable, why not the Branches?

FAINALL.   So, so, why this point's clear,——Well how do we   635 proceed?

MRS MARWOOD.   I will contrive a Letter which shall be deliver'd to my Lady at the time when that Rascal who is to act Sir *Rowland* is with her. It shall come as from an unknown hand ——for the less I appear to know of the truth——the better I   640 can play the Incendiary. Besides I would not have *Foible* provok'd if I cou'd help it,——because you know she knows some pas- sages——Nay I expect all will come out——But let the Mine be sprung first, and then I care not if I'm discover'd.

FAINALL.   If the worst come to the worst,——I'll turn my Wife   645 to Grass——I have already a deed of Settlement of the best part of her Estate; which I wheadl'd out of her; And that you shall partake at least.

MRS MARWOOD. I hope you are convinc'd that I hate *Mirabell*, now you'll be no more Jealous.   650

FAINALL. Jealous no,——By this Kiss——let Husbands be Jealous; But let the Lover still believe. Or if he doubt, let it be only to endear his pleasure, and prepare the Joy that follows, when he proves his Mistress true; but let Husbands doubts Convert to endless Jealousie; or if they have belief, let it Corrupt   655 to Superstitition, and blind Credulity. I am single; and will herd no more with 'em. True, I wear the badge; but I'll disown the Order. And since I take my leave of 'em, I care not if I leave 'em a common Motto, to their common Crest.

> *All Husbands must, or pain, or shame, endure;*   660
> *The Wise too Jealous are, Fools too secure.*

> > *Exeunt.*

ACT IV

SCENE I

Scene Continues

Enter LADY WISHFORT *and* FOIBLE.

LADY WISHFORT. Is Sir *Rowland* coming say'st thou, *Foible*? and are things in Order?

FOIBLE. Yes, *Madam*. I have put Wax-Lights in the Sconces; and plac'd the Foot-men in a Row in the Hall, in their best Liveries, with the Coach-man and Postilion to fill up the   5 Equipage.

LADY WISHFORT. Have you pullvill'd the Coach-man and Postilion, that they may not stink of the Stable, when Sir *Rowland* comes by?

FOIBLE. Yes, *Madam*.   10

LADY WISHFORT. And are the Dancers and the Musick ready, that he may be entertain'd in all points with Correspondence to his Passion?

FOIBLE. All is ready, *Madam*.

LADY WISHFORT. And——well——and how do I look, 15
Foible?

FOIBLE. Most killing well, Madam.

LADY WISHFORT. Well, and how shall I receive him? In what
figure shall I give his Heart the first Impression? There is a great
deal in the first Impression. Shall I sit?——No I won't sit—— 20
I'll walk——aye I'll walk from the door upon his entrance; and
then turn full upon him——No, that will be too sudden. I'll lie
——aye, I'll lie down——I'll receive him in my little dressing
Room, there's a Couch——Yes, yes, I'll give the first impression
on a Couch——I wont lie neither but loll and lean upon one 25
Elbow; with one Foot a little dangling off, Jogging in a thought-
ful way——Yes——and then as soon as he appears, start, ay,
start and be surpriz'd, and rise to meet him in a pretty disorder
——Yes——O, nothing is more alluring than a Levee from a
Couch in some Confusion.——It shews the Foot to advantage, 30
and furnishes with Blushes, and re-composing Airs beyond
Comparison. Hark! There's a Coach.

FOIBLE. 'Tis he, Madam.

LADY WISHFORT. O dear, has my Nephew made his Addresses
to Millamant? I order'd him. 35

FOIBLE. Sir Wilfull is set in to Drinking, Madam, in the Parlour.

LADY WISHFORT. Ods my life, I'll send him to her. Call her
down, Foible; bring her hither. I'll send him as I go——When
they are together, then comes to me Foible, that I may not be too
long alone with Sir Rowland. 40

Exit.

Enter MILLAMANT, *and* MRS FAINALL.

FOIBLE. Madam, I stay'd here, to tell your Ladyship that Mr.
Mirabell has waited this half hour for an Opportunity to talk with
you. Tho' my Lady's Orders were to leave you and Sir Wilfull
together. Shall I tell Mr. Mirabell that you are at leisure?

MILLAMANT. No——What would the Dear man have? I am 45
thoughtfull and would amuse my self,——bid him come another
time.

Repeating and Walking about.

There never yet was Woman made,
Nor shall but to be curs'd.

That's hard! 50

MRS FAINALL. You are very fond of Sir *John Suckling* to day, *Millamant*, and the *Poets*.

MILLAMANT. He? Ay, and filthy Verses——So I am.

FOIBLE. Sir *Wilfull* is coming, *Madam*. Shall I send Mr. *Mirabell* away? 55

MILLAMANT. Ay, if you please *Foible*, send him away,—— Or send him hither,——just as you will Dear *Foible*.——I think I'll see him——Shall I? Ay, let the Wretch come.

Repeating.

Thyrsis a Youth of the Inspir'd train——

Dear *Fainall*, Entertain Sir *Wilfull*——Thou hast Philosophy 60 to undergo a Fool, thou art Married and hast Patience—— I would confer with my own Thoughts.

MRS FAINALL. I am oblig'd to you, that you would make me your Proxy in this Affair; but I have business of my own.

Enter SIR WILFULL.

O Sir *Wilfull*; you are come at the Critical Instant. There's your 65 Mistress up to the Ears in Love and Contemplation, pursue your Point, now or never.

SIR WILFULL. Yes; my Aunt would have it so,——I would gladly have been encouraged with a Bottle or two, because I'm somewhat wary at first, before I am acquainted;——But I hope 70 after a time, I shall break my mind——that is upon further acquaintance,——So for the present Cosen, I'll take my leave ——If so be you'll be so kind to make my Excuse, I'll return to my Company——

This while MILLAMANT *walks about Repeating to her self.*

MRS FAINALL. O fie Sir *Wilfull*! What, you must not be 75 Daunted.

SIR WILFULL. Daunted, No, that's not it, it is not so much for that——for if so be that I set on't, I'll do't. But only for the present, 'tis sufficient till further acquaintance, that's all——your Servant. 80

MRS FAINALL. Nay, I'll swear you shall never lose so

favourable an opportunity, if I can help it. I'll leave you together and lock the Door.

Exit.

SIR WILFULL.   Nay, nay Cozen,——I have forgot my Gloves,
——What dee do? 'Shart a'has lock'd the Door indeed I think——   85
Nay Cozen *Fainall*, open the Door——Pshaw, What a Vixon
trick is this?——Nay, now a'has seen me too——Cozen, I made
bold to pass thro' as it were,——I think this Door's In-
chanted——

MILLAMANT.   *Repeating.*

> *I prithee spare me gentle Boy,*   90
> *Press me no more for that slight Toy.*

SIR WILFULL.   Anan? Cozen, your Servant.
MILLAMANT.——*That foolish trifle of a heart*——Sir *Wilfull*!
SIR WILFULL.   Yes,——your Servant. No offence I hope,
Cozen.   95
MILLAMANT.   *Repeating.*

> *I swear it will not do its part,*
> *Tho' thou do'st thine, employ'st thy Power and Art.*

Natural, easie *Suckling*!
SIR WILFULL.   Anan? *Suckling?* No such Suckling neither,
Cozen, nor Stripling: I thank Heav'n, I'm no Minor.   100
MILLAMANT.   Ah Rustick! ruder than *Gothick*.
SIR WILFULL.   Well, Well, I shall understand your *Lingo* one
of these days, Cozen, in the mean while, I must answer in plain
English.
MILLAMANT.   Have you any business with me, Sir *Wilfull?*   105
SIR WILFULL.   Not at present Cozen,——Yes, I made bold to
see, to come and know if that how you were dispos'd to fetch a
walk this Evening, if so be that I might not be troublesome, I
wou'd have fought a walk with you.
MILLAMANT.   A walk? What then?   110
SIR WILFULL.   Nay nothing——Only for the walks sake, that's
all——
MILLAMANT.   I Nauseate walking; 'tis a Country diversion, I
loath the Country and every thing that relates to it.

SIR WILFULL.   Indeed! Hah! Look ye, you do? Nay, 'tis like   115
you may——Here are choice of Pastimes here in Town, as Plays
and the like that must be confess'd indeed.——

MILLAMANT.   *Ah l'etourdie*! I hate the Town too.

SIR WILFULL.   Dear Heart, that's much——Hah! that you
shou'd hate 'em both! Hah! 'tis like you may; there are some   120
can't relish the Town, and others can't away with the Country,
——'tis like you may be one of those, Cozen.

MILLAMANT.   Ha, ha, ha. Yes, 'tis like I may.——You have
nothing further to say to me?

SIR WILFULL.   Not at present, Cozen.——'tis like when I have   125
an Opportunity to be more private,——I may break my mind in
some measure,——I conjecture you partly guess——However
that's as time shall try,——But spare to speak and spare to speed,
as they say.

MILLAMANT.   If it is of no great Importance, Sir *Wilfull*, you   130
will oblige me to leave me: I have just now a little business.——

SIR WILFULL.   Enough, enough, Cozen, Yes, yes, all a case
——When you're dispos'd, when you're dispos'd. Now's as
well as another time; and another time as well as now. All's one
for that,——yes, yes, if you Concerns call you, there's no hast;   135
it will keep cold as they say,——Cosen, your Servant,
I think this door's lock'd.

MILLAMANT.   You may go this way Sir.

SIR WILFULL.   Your Servant, then with your leave I'll return
to my Company.   140

Exit.

MILLAMANT.   Ay, ay, ha, ha, ha.

Like Phœbus *sung the no less am'rous Boy.*

Enter MIRABELL.

MIRABELL.   ——*Like* Daphne *she as lovely and as Coy.*
Do you lock your self up from me, to make my search more
Curious? Or is this pretty Artifice Contriv'd, to Signifie that here   145
the Chase must end, and my pursuit to Crown'd, for you can fly
no further.——

MILLAMANT.   Vanity! No——I'll fly and be follow'd to the last
moment, tho' I am upon the very Verge of Matrimony; I expect

you shou'd solicite me as much as if I were wavering at the grate   150
of a Monastery, with one foot over the threshold. I'll be solicited
to the very last, nay and afterwards.

MIRABELL.   What, after the last?

MILLAMANT.   O, I should think I was poor and had nothing to
bestow, If I were reduc'd to an Inglorious ease; and free'd from   155
the Agreeable fatigues of solicitation.

MIRABELL.   But do not you know, that when favours are con-
ferr'd upon Instant and tedious Sollicitation, that they diminish
in their value, and that both the giver loses the grace, and the
receiver lessens his Pleasure?   160

MILLAMANT.   It may be in things of common Application; but
never sure in Love. O, I hate a Lover, that can dare to think, he
draws a moments air, Independent on the Bounty of his Mistress.
There is not so Impudent a thing in Nature, as the sawcy look of
an assured man, Confident of Success. The Pedantick arrogance   165
of a very Husband, has not so Pragmatical an Air. Ah! I'll never
marry, unless I am first made sure of my will and pleasure.

MIRABELL.   Wou'd you have 'em both before Marriage? Or will
you be contented with the first now, and stay for the other till
after grace?   170

MILLAMANT.   Ah don't be Impertinent——My dear Liberty, shall
I leave thee? My faithful Solitude, my darling Contemplation
must I bid you then Adieu? ay–h adieu.——my morning
thoughts, agreeable wakings, indolent slumbers, all ye
douceurs, ye *Someils du Matin adieu*——I can't do't, 'tis more   175
than Impossible——positively *Mirabel*, I'll lie a Bed in a morning
as long as I please.

MIRABELL.   Then I'll get up in a morning as early as I please.

MILLAMANT.   Ah! Idle Creature, get up when you will—and,
dee hear, I won't be call'd names after I'm Married; positively I   180
won't be call'd Names.

MIRABELL.   Names!

MILLAMANT.   Ay as Wife, Spouse, My dear, Joy, Jewel, Love,
Sweet heart and the rest of that Nauseous Cant, in which Men
and their Wives are so fulsomely familiar,——I shall never bear   185
that,——Good *Mirabell* don't let us be familiar or fond, nor kiss
before folks, like my Lady *Fadler* and Sir *Francis*: Nor goe to
Hide-Park together the first *Sunday* in a New Chariot, to provoke

Eyes and Whispers; and then never to be seen there together again; as if we were proud of one another the first Week, and asham'd of one another for ever After. Let us never Visit together, nor go to a Play together, But let us be very strange and well bred: let us be as strange as if we had been married a great while; and as well bred as if we were not marri'd at all.

MIRABELL.   Have you any more Conditions to offer? Hitherto your demands are pretty reasonable.

MILLAMANT.   Trifles,——As liberty to pay and receive visits to and from whom I please, write and receive Letters, without Interrogatories or wry Faces on your part. To wear what I please; and choose Conversation with regard only to my own taste; to have no obligation upon me to converse with Wits that I don't like, because they are your acquaintance; or to be intimate with Fools, because they may be your Relations. Come to Dinner when I please, dine in my dressing room when I'm out of humour without giving a reason. To have my Closet Inviolate; to be sole Empress of my Tea-table, which you must never presume to approach without first asking leave. And lastly, where ever I am, you shall always knock at the door before you come in. These Articles subscrib'd, If I continue to endure you a little longer, I may by degrees dwindle into a Wife.

MIRABELL.   Your bill of fare is something advanc'd in this latter account. Well, have I Liberty to offer Conditions——that when you are dwindl'd into a Wife, I may not be beyond Measure enlarg'd into a Husband?

MILLAMANT.   You have free leave; propose your utmost, speak and spare not.

MIRABELL.   I thank you. *Inprimis* then, I Covenant that your acquaintance be General; that you admit no sworn Confident, or Intimate of your own Sex; No she friend to skreen her affairs under your Countenance and tempt you to make tryal of a Mutual Secresie. No Decoy-Duck to wheadle you a *fop*—— *scrambling* to the Play in a Mask——then bring you home in a pretended fright, when you think you shall be found out.—— And rail at me for missing the Play, and disappointing the Frolick which you had to pick me up and prove my Constancy.

MILLAMANT.   Detestable *Inprimis*! I go to the Play in a Mask!

MIRABELL.   *Item*, I Article, that you continue to like your own

Face, as long as I shall. And while it passes Current with me, that
you endeavour not to new Coin it. To which end, together with
all Vizards for the day, I prohibit all Masks for the Night, made of   230
oil'd-skins and I know not what——Hog's-bones, Hare's-gall,
Pig-water, and the marrow of a roasted Cat. In short, I forbid all
Commerce with the Gentlewoman in *what-de-call-it*-Court. *Item*,
I shut my doors against all Bauds with Baskets, and penny-worths
of *Muslin, China, Fans, Atlases,* &c.——*Item* when you shall   235
be Breeding——

MILLAMANT.   Ah! Name it not.

MIRABELL.   Which may be presum'd, with a blessing on our
endeavours——

MILLAMANT.   Odious endeavours!   240

MIRABELL.   I denounce against all strait-Laceing, Squeezing for
a Shape, till you mold my boy's head like a Sugar-Loaf, and
instead of a Man-child, make me the Father to a Crooked-billet.
Lastly to the Dominion of the *Tea-table*, I submit.——But with
proviso, that you exceed not in your province; but restrain your   245
self to Native and Simple *Tea-Table* drinks, as *Tea, Chocolate* and
Coffee. As likewise to Genuine and, Authoriz'd *Tea-Table* talk,
——such as mending of Fashions, spoiling Reputations, railing
at absent Friends, and so forth——but that on no account you
encroach upon the mens prerogative, and presume to drink   250
healths, or toste fellows; for prevention of which, I banish all
Foreign Forces, all Auxiliaries to the *Tea-Table,* as *Orange-
Brandy,* all *Anniseed, Cinamon, Citron* and *Barbado*'s-*Waters,*
together with *Ratifia* and the most noble Spirit of *Clary,*——
but for *Couslip-Wine, Poppy-Water* and all *Dormitives,* those I   255
allow,——these *proviso*'s admitted, in other things I may prove
a tractable and complying Husband.

MILLAMANT.   O horrid *proviso*'s! filthy strong Waters! I toste
fellows, Odious Men! I hate your Odious *proviso*'s.

MIRABELL.   Then wee're agreed. Shall I kiss your hand upon the   260
Contract? and here comes one to be a witness to the Sealing of the
Deed.

Enter MRS FAINALL.

MILLAMANT.   *Fainall,* what shall I do? shall I have him? I think
I must have him.

MRS FAINALL.   Ay, ay, take him, take him, what shou'd you   265
do?

MILLAMANT.   Well then——I'll take my death I'm in a horrid
fright——*Fainall*, I shall never say it——well——I think——
I'll endure you.

MRS FAINALL.   Fy, fy, have him, have him, and tell him so in   270
plain terms: For I am sure you have a mind to him.

MILLAMANT.   Are you? I think I have——and the horrid Man
looks as if he thought so too——Well, you ridiculous thing you,
I'll have you,——I won't be kiss'd, nor I won't be thank'd——
here kiss my hand tho'——so hold your tongue now, and don't   275
say a word.

MRS FAINALL.   *Mirabell*, there's a Necessity for your obedience;
——You have neither time to talk nor stay. My Mother is
coming; and in my Conscience if she should see you, wou'd fall
into fits, and maybe not recover time enough to return to Sir   280
Rowland, who as *Foible* tells me is in a fair way to succeed. Therefore spare your Extacies for another occasion, and slip down the
back-stairs, where *Foible* waits to consult you.

MILLAMANT.   Ay, go, go. In the mean time I suppose you have
said something to please me.   285

MIRABELL.   I am all Obedience.

Exit MIRABELL.

MRS FAINALL.   Yonder Sir *Wilfull*'s Drunk; and so noisy that
my Mother has been forc'd to leave Sir *Rowland* to appease him;
But he answers her only with Singing and Drinking——what
they have done by this time I know not. But *Petulant* and he were   290
upon quarelling as I came by.

MILLAMANT.   Well, If *Mirabell* shou'd not make a good Husband, I am a lost thing;——for I find I love him violently.

MRS FAINALL.   So it seems, when you mind not what's said to
you,——If you doubt him, you had best take up with Sir *Wilfull*.   295

MILLAMANT.   How can you name that super-annuated Lubber,
foh!

Enter WITWOUD *from drinking*.

MRS FAINALL.   So, Is the fray made up, that you have left 'em?

WITWOUD.   Left 'em? I cou'd stay no longer——I have laugh'd

like ten Christnings——I am tipsy with laughing——If I had 300
staid any longer I should have burst,——I must have been let
out and piec'd in the sides like an unsiz'd Camlet,——Yes, yes
the fray is compos'd; my Lady came in like a *Noli prosequi* and
stop't their proceedings.

MILLAMANT.   What was the dispute?   305

WITWOUD.   That's the Jest, there was no dispute, they cou'd
neither of 'em speak for rage; And so fell a sputt'ring at one
another like two roasting Apples.

Enter PETULANT *Drunk.*

Now *Petulant*, all's over, all's well; Gad my head begins to
whim it about——Why dost thou not speak? thou art both as 310
drunk and as mute as a Fish.

PETULANT.   Look you Mrs. *Millamant*,——If you can love me
dear Nymph——say it——and that's the Conclusion——pass
on, or pass off,——that's all.

WITWOUD.   Thou hast utter'd *Volumes*, *Folio's*, in less than 315
Decimo Sexto, my Dear *Lacedemonian*, Sirrah *Petulant*, thou art
an Epitomizer of words.

PETULANT.   *Witwou'd*——You are an anihilator of sense.

WITWOUD.   Thou art a retailer of Phrases; and dost deal in
Remnants of Remnants, like a maker of Pincushions——thou 320
art in truth (Metaphorically speaking) A speaker of shorthand.

PETULANT.   Thou art (without a figure) Just one half of an Ass;
and *Baldwin* yonder, thy half Brother is the rest——A *gemini* of
Asses split, would make just four of you.

WITWOUD.   Thou dost bite my dear Mustard-seed; kiss me for 325
that.

PETULANT.   Stand off——I'll kiss no more Males,——I have
kiss'd your *twin* yonder in a humour of reconciliation, till he
[*hiccup*] rises upon my stomack like a Radish.

MILLAMANT.   Eh! filthy creature——what was the quarrel?   330

PETULANT.   There was no quarrel——there might have been a
quarrel.

WITWOUD.   If there had been words enow between 'em to have
express'd provocation; they had gone together by the Ears like
a pair of Castanets.   335

PETULANT.   You were the Quarrel.

MILLAMANT. Me!

PETULANT. If I have a humour to Quarrel, I can make less
matters conclude Premises,——If you are not handsom, what
then? If I have a humour to prove it.——If I shall have my   340
Reward, say so; if not, fight for your Face the next time your
self——I'll go sleep.

WITWOUD. Do, wrap thy self up like a *Wood-louse* and dream
Revenge——and hear me, if thou canst learn to write by tomorrow Morning, Pen me a Challenge——I'll carry it for thee.   345

PETULANT. Carry your Mistresses *Monkey* a *Spider*,——go flea
Dogs, and read Romances——I'll go to bed to my Maid.

Exit.

MRS FAINALL. He's horribly drunk——how came you all in
this pickle?——

WITWOUD. A plot, a plot, to get rid of the Knight,——your   350
Husband's advice; but he sneak'd off.

Enter LADY WISHFORT *and* SIR WILFULL *drunk.*

LADY WISHFORT. Out upon't, out upon't, at years of Discretion, and Comport your self at this Rantipole rate.

SIR WILFULL. No Offence Aunt.

LADY WISHFORT. Offence? As I'm a Person, I'm asham'd of   355
you,——Fogh! how you stink of Wine! Dee think my Neice
will ever endure such a *Borachio*! you'r an absolute *Borachio*.

SIR WILFULL. *Borachio*!

LADY WISHFORT. At a time when you shou'd commence an
Amour and put your best foot foremost——   360

SIR WILFULL. 'Sheart, an you grutch me your Liquor, make a
Bill——Give me more drink and take my Purse.

Sings.

> *Prithee fill me the Glass*
> *Till it laugh in my Face,*
> *With Ale that is Potent and Mellow;*   365
> *He that Whines for a Lass,*
> *Is an Ignorant Ass,*
> *For a* Bumper *has not its Fellow.*

But if you wou'd have me Marry my Cosen,——say the Word,
and I'll do't——*Wilfull* will do't, that's the Word——*Wilfull* 370
will do't, that's my Crest——my Motto I have forgot.

LADY WISHFORT.   My Nephew's a little overtaken Cosen——
but 'tis with drinking your Health——O' my Word you are
oblig'd to him.

SIR WILFULL.   *In vino veritas* Aunt,——If I drunk your 375
Health to day Cosen——I am a *Borachio*. But if you have a mind
to be Marry'd, say the Word, and send for the Piper, *Wilfull*
will do't. If not, dust it away, and let's have tother round——
Tony, Ods heart where's *Tony*——*Tony's* an honest fellow, but
he spits after a Bumper, and that's a Fault.   380

Sings.

> *We'll drink and we'll never ha' done Boys*
> *Put the glass then around with the Sun Boys*
> *Let* Apollo's *Example invite us;*
> *For he's drunk every Night,*
> *And that makes him so bright,*   385
> *That he's able next Morning to light us.*

The Sun's a good Pimple, an honest Soaker, he has a Cellar at
your *Antipodes*. If I travel Aunt, I touch at your *Antipodes*——
your *Antipodes* are a good rascally sort of topsy turvy Fellows
——If I had a Bumper I'd stand upon my Head and drink a 390
Health to 'em——A Match or no Match, Cosen, with the hard
Name,——Aunt, *Wilfull* will do't. If she has her Maidenhead let
her look to't,——if she has not, let her keep her own Counsel in
the mean time, and cry out at the nine Months end.

MILLAMANT.   Your Pardon Madam, I can stay no longer—— 395
Sir *Wilfull* grows very powerful, Egh! how he smells! I shall be
overcome if I stay. Come, Cosen.

Exeunt MILLAMANT *and* MRS FAINALL.

LADY WISHFORT. Smells! he would poison a Tallow-
Chandler and his Family. Beastly Creature, I know not what to
do with him——Travel quoth a; Ay travel, travel, get thee gone, 400
get thee but far enough, to the *Saracens* or the *Tartars*, or the
Turks——for thou are not fit to live in a Christian Common-
wealth, thou beastly Pagan,

SIR WILFULL. *Turks*, no; no *Turks*, Aunt: Your *Turks* are
Infidels, and believe not in the Grape. Your *Mahometan*, your   405
Mussulman is a dry Stinkard——No Offence, Aunt. My Map
says that your *Turk* is not so honest a Man as your Christian——
I cannot find by the Map that your *Mufti* is Orthodox——
Whereby it is plain Case, that Orthodox is a hard Word, Aunt,
and [*hiccup*] Greek for Claret.   410

Sings.

> To drink is a Christian Diversion,
> Unknown to the Turk and the Persian:
>   Let Mahometan Fools
>   Live by Heathenish Rules,
> And be damn'd over Tea-Cups and Coffee.   415
>   But let British Lads sing,
>   Crown a Health to the King,
> And a Fig for your Sultan and Sophy.
> Ah *Tony*!

Enter FOIBLE, *and whispers* LADY WISHFORT.

LADY WISHFORT. Sir *Rowland* impatient? Good lack! what   420
shall I do with this beastly Tumbril?——Go lie down and sleep,
you Sot——Or as I'm a person, I'll have you bastinado'd with
Broom-sticks. Call up the Wenches.

Exit FOIBLE.

SIR WILFULL. Ahey! Wenches, where are the Wenches?
LADY WISHFORT. Dear Cosen *Witwou'd*, get him away, and   425
you will bind me to you inviolably. I have an Affair of moment
that invades me with some precipitation——You will oblige me
to all Futurity.
WITWOUD. Come Knight——Pox on him. I don't know what
to say to him——will you go to a Cock-match?   430
SIR WILFULL. With a Wench, *Tony*? Is she a shake-bag Sirrah?
let me bite your Cheek for that.
WITWOUD. Horrible! He has a breath like a *Bagpipe*——ay, ay,
come will you March my *Salopian*?
SIR WILFULL. Lead on little *Tony*——I'll follow thee my   435

Anthony, My *Tantony*, Sirrah thou sha't be my *Tantony*; and I'll
be thy *Pig*.
——*And a fig for your* Sultan *and* Sophy.

Exit Singing with WITWOUD.

LADY WISHFORT. This will never do. It will never make a
Match.——At least before he has been abroad.   440

Enter WAITWELL, *disguis'd as for* SIR ROWLAND.

Dear Sir *Rowland*, I am Confounded with Confusion at the
Retrospection of my own rudeness,——I have more pardons to
ask than the *Pope* distributes in the Year of *Jubilee*. But I hope
where there is likely to be so near an alliance,——We may un-
bend the severity of *Decorum*——and dispence with a little   445
Ceremony.

WAITWELL. My Impatience *Madam*, is the effect of my
transport,——and till I have the possession of your adoreable
Person, I am tantaliz'd on a rack; And do but hang *Madam*, on
the tenter of Expectation.   450

LADY WISHFORT. You have Excess of gallantry Sir *Rowland*;
and press things to a Conclusion, with a most prevailing Vehemence.——But a day or two for decency of Marriage——

WAITWELL. For decency of Funeral, *Madam*. The delay will
break my heart——or if that should fail, I shall be Poyson'd. 455
My *Nephew* will get an inkling of my Designs and Poison me,
——and I wou'd willingly starve him before I die——I wou'd
gladly go out of the World with that Satisfaction.——That
wou'd be some Comfort to me, If I cou'd but live so long as to be
reveng'd on that Unnatural *Viper*.   460

LADY WISHFORT. Is he so Unnatural say you? truely I wou'd
Contribute much both to the saving of your Life; and the
accomplishment of your revenge——Not that I respect my self;
tho' he has been a perfidious wretch to me.

WAITWELL. Perfidious to you!   465

LADY WISHFORT. O Sir *Rowland*, the hours that he has dy'd
away at my Feet, the Tears that he has shed, the Oaths that he has
sworn, the Palpitations that he has felt, the Trances, and the
Tremblings, the Ardors and the Ecstacies, the Kneelings and the

Riseings, the Heart-heavings and the hand-Gripings, the Pangs   470
and the Pathetick Regards of his protesting Eyes! Oh no memory
can Register.

WAITWELL.   What, my Rival! is the Rebell my Rival? a'dies.

LADY WISHFORT.   No, don't kill him at once Sir *Rowland*,
starve him gradually inch by inch.   475

WAITWELL.   I'll do't. In three weeks he shall be bare-foot; in a
month out at knees with begging an *Alms*,——he shall starve upward and upward, till he has nothing living but his head, and then
go out in a stink like a Candle's end upon a Save-all.

LADY WISHFORT.   Well, Sir *Rowland*, you have the way,——   480
You are no Novice in the Labyrinth of Love——You have the
Clue——But as I am a person, Sir *Rowland*, You must not attri-
bute my yielding to any sinister appetite, or Indigestion of
Widdow-hood; Nor Impute my Complacency, to any Lethargy
of Continence——I hope you do not think me prone to any   485
iteration of Nuptials.——

WAITWELL.   Far be it from me——

LADY WISHFORT.   If you do, I protest I must recede——or
think that I have made a prostitution of decorums, but in the
Vehemence of Compassion, and to save the life of a Person of so   490
much Importance——

WAITWELL.   I esteem it so——

LADY WISHFORT.   Or else you wrong my Condescension——

WAITWELL.   I do not, I do not——

LADY WISHFORT.   Indeed you do.   495

WAITWELL.   I do not, fair shrine of Vertue.

LADY WISHFORT.   If you think the least scruple of Carnality
was an Ingredient——

WAITWELL.   Dear *Madam*, no. You are all *Camphire* and
Frankincense, all *Chastity* and *Odour*.   500

LADY WISHFORT.   Or that——

Enter FOIBLE.

FOIBLE.   *Madam*, the Dancers are ready, and there's one with a
Letter, who must deliver it into your own hands.

LADY WISHFORT.   Sir *Rowland*, will you give me leave? think
favourably, Judge Candidly and conclude you have found a   505

Person who wou'd suffer racks in honour's cause, dear Sir
Rowland, and will wait on you Incessantly.

Exit.

WAITWELL. Fie, fie!——What a Slavery have I undergone;
Spouse, hast thou any *Cordial*——I want *Spirits*.

FOIBLE. What a washy Rogue art thou, to pant thus for a   510
quarter of an hours lying and swearing to a fine Lady?

WAITWELL. O, she is the *Antidote* to desire. Spouse, thou will't
fare the worse for't——I shall have no appetite to iteration of
Nuptials——this eight and fourty Hours——by this hand I'd
rather be a *Chair-man* in the *Dog-days*——than Act Sir *Rowland*,   515
till this time tomorrow.

Enter LADY WISHFORT *with a Letter.*

LADY WISHFORT. Call in the *Dancers*;——Sir *Rowland*, we'll
sit if you please, and see the Entertainment.

Dance.

Now with your permission Sir *Rowland* I will peruse my Letter
——I wou'd open it in your presence, because I wou'd not make   520
you Uneasie. If it shou'd make you Uneasie I wou'd burn it——
speak if it do's——but you may see by the Superscription it is like
a Woman's hand.

FOIBLE. By Heaven! Mrs. *Marwood*'s, I know it,——my heart
akes——[*to him*] get it from her——   525

WAITWELL. A Woman's hand? No *Madam*, that's no Woman's
hand I see that already. That's some body whose throat must be
cut.

LADY WISHFORT. Nay Sir *Rowland*, since you give me a proof
of your Passion by your Jealousie, I promise you I'll make you a   530
return, by a frank Communication——You shall see it——
wee'll open it together——look you here.

[*Reads.*]——Madam, *tho' unknown to you* (Look you there 'tis
from no body that I know)——*I have that honour for your
Character, that I think my self oblig'd to let you know you are abus'd.*   535
He who pretends to be Sir Rowland *is a cheat and a Rascal.*——
Oh Heavens! what's this?

FOIBLE. Unfortunate, all's ruin'd.

WAITWELL. How, how, Let me see, let me see——[*reading*]
    A Rascal and disguis'd and subborn'd for that imposture,——O   540
    villany! O villany!——*by the Contrivance of*——

LADY WISHFORT. I shall faint, I shall die, I shall die, oh!

FOIBLE. Say 'tis your Nephew's hand.——[*to him*] quickly, his
    plot, swear, swear it.——

WAITWELL. Here's a Villain! *Madam*, don't you perceive it,   545
    don't you see it?

LADY WISHFORT. Too well, too well. I have seen too much.

WAITWELL. I told you at first I knew the hand——A Woman's
    hand? the Rascal writes a sort of a large hand; your *Roman* hand
    ——I saw there was a throat to be cut presently. If he were my   550
    Son as he is my Nephew I'd Pistoll him——

FOIBLE. O Treachery! But are you sure Sir *Rowland*, it is his
    writing?

WAITWELL. Sure? am I here? do I live? do I love this Pearl of
    India? I have twenty Letters in my Pocket from him, in the same   555
    Character.

LADY WISHFORT. How!

FOIBLE. O what luck it is Sir *Rowland*, that you were present at
    this Juncture! this was the business that brought Mr. *Mirabell*
    disguis'd to *Madam Millamant* this Afternoon. I thought some-   560
    thing was contriving, when he stole by me and would have hid
    his face.

LADY WISHFORT. How, how!——I heard the Villain was in
    the house indeed, and now I remember, my *Niece* went away
    abruptly, when Sir *Wilfull* was to have made his addresses.   565

FOIBLE. Then, then *Madam*, Mr. *Mirabell* waited for her in her
    Chamber, but I wou'd not tell your Lady-ship to discompose you
    when you were to receive Sir *Rowland*.

WAITWELL. Enough, his date is short.

FOIBLE. No, good Sir *Rowland*, don't incurr the Law.   570

WAITWELL. Law? I care not for Law. I can but die, and 'tis in a
    good cause——my Lady shall be satisfied of my Truth and
    Innocence, tho' it cost me my life.

LADY WISHFORT. No, dear Sir *Rowland*, don't fight, if you
    shou'd be kill'd I must never shew my face; or hang'd,——O   575
    Consider my Reputation Sir *Rowland*——No you shan't fight,

——I'll go in and Examine my *Niece*; I'll make her Confess. I
conjure you Sir *Rowland* by all your love not to fight.

WAITWELL.   I am Charm'd *Madam*, I obey. But some proof you
must let me give you;——I'll go for a black box, which Contains   580
the Writings of my whole Estate, and deliver that into your
hands.

LADY WISHFORT.   Ay dear Sir *Rowland*, that will be some
Comfort; bring the Black-box.

WAITWELL.   And may I presume to bring a Contract to be sign'd   585
this Night? May I hope so farr?

LADY WISHFORT.   Bring what you will; but come alive, pray
come alive. O this is a happy discovery.

WAITWELL.   Dead or Alive I'll come——and married we will
be in spight of treachery; Ay and get an Heir that shall defeat the   590
last remaining glimpse of hope in my abandon'd *Nephew*. Come
my Buxom Widdow.

> *Ere long you shall Substantial proof receive*
> *That I'm an Arrant Knight*——

FOIBLE.   *Or arrant Knave.*   595

> *Exeunt.*

ACT V

SCENE I

Scene Continues

LADY WISHFORT *and* FOIBLE.

LADY WISHFORT.   Out of my house, out of my house, thou
Viper, thou *Serpent*, that I have foster'd, thou bosome traytress,
that I rais'd from nothing——begon, begon, begon, go, go,——
that I took from Washing of old Gause and Weaving of dead
Hair, with a bleak blew Nose, over a Chafeing-dish of starv'd   5
Embers and Dining behind a Traver's Rag, in a shop no bigger
than a Bird-cage,——go, go, starve again, do, do.

FOIBLE.   Dear *Madam*, I'll beg pardon on my knees.

LADY WISHFORT. Away, out, out, go set up for your self
again——do, drive a Trade, do, with your three penny worth of   10
small Ware, flaunting upon a Packthread, under a Brandy-sellers
Bulk, or against a dead Wall by a Ballad-monger. Go hang out an
old *Frisoneer-gorget*, with a yard of Yellow *Colberteen* again; do;
an old gnaw'd *Mask*, two rowes of *Pins* and a *Childs Fiddle*;
A *Glass Necklace* with the Beads broken, and a *Quilted Night-cap*   15
with one Ear. Go, go, drive a trade,——these were your *Com-
modities* you treacherous Trull, this was the *Merchandize* you dealt
in, when I took you into my house, plac'd you next my self, And
made you Governante of my whole Family. You have forgot this,
have you? Now you have feather'd your Nest.   20

FOIBLE. No, no, dear *Madam*. Do but hear me, have but a
Moment's patience——I'll Confess all. Mr. *Mirabell* seduc'd me;
I am not the first that he has wheadl'd with his dissembling
Tongue; Your Lady-ship's own Wisdom has been deluded by
him, then how shou'd I a poor Ignorant, defend my self? O   25
Madam, If you knew but what he promis'd me; and how he
assur'd me your Ladyship shou'd come to no damage——Or
else the Wealth of the *Indies* shou'd not have brib'd me to con-
spire against so Good, so Sweet, so kind a Lady as you have been
to me.   30

LADY WISHFORT. No damage? What to Betray me, to Marry
me to a Cast-serving-man; to make me a receptacle, an Hospital
for a decay'd Pimp? No damage? O thou frontless Impudence,
more than a big-Belly'd Actress.

FOIBLE.   Pray do but hear me *Madam*, he cou'd not marry your   35
Lady-ship, *Madam*——No indeed his Marriage was to have been
void in Law; for he was married to me first, to secure your Ladyship. He cou'd not have bedded your Lady-ship: for if he had
Consummated with your Lady-ship, he must have run the
risque of the Law, and been put upon his *Clergy*——Yes indeed,   40
I enquir'd of the Law in that case before I wou'd meddle or make.

LADY WISHFORT.   What, then I have been your Property, have
I? I have been convenient to you it seems,——while you were
Catering for *Mirabell*; I have been broker for you? What, have
you made a passive Bawd of me?——this Exceeds all precedent;   45
I am brought to fine uses, to become a botcher of second hand
Marriages, between *Abigails* and *Andrews*! I'll couple you, Yes,

I'll baste you together, you and your *Philander*. I'll *Dukes-Place*
you, as I'm a Person. Your Turtle is in Custody already; You
shall Coo in the same Cage, if there be Constable or warrant in   50
the Parish.

Exit.

FOIBLE.   O that ever I was Born, O that I was ever Married,——
a Bride, ay I shall be a *Bridewell*-Bride. Oh!

Enter MRS FAINALL.

MRS FAINALL.   Poor *Foible*, what's the matter?

FOIBLE.   *O Madam*, my Lady's gone for a Constable; I shall be   55
had to a Justice, and put to *Bridewell* to beat Hemp, poor *Waitwell's* gone to prison already.

MRS FAINALL.   Have a good heart *Foible*, *Mirabell's* gone to
give security for him, this is all *Marwood's* and my Husband's
doing.   60

FOIBLE.   Yes, yes; I know it *Madam*; she was in my Lady's
Closet, and over-heard all that you said to me before Dinner. She
sent the Letter to my Lady, and that missing Effect, Mr. *Fainall*
laid this Plot to arrest *Waitwell*, when he pretended to go for the
Papers; and in the mean-time Mrs. *Marwood* declar'd all to my   65
Lady.

MRS FAINALL.   Was there no mention of me in the Letter?
——My Mother do's not suspect my being in the Confederacy?
I fancy *Marwood* has not told her, tho' she has told my husband.

FOIBLE.   Yes *Madam*; but my Lady did not see that part; We   70
stifl'd the Letter before she read so far. Has that mischeivous
Devil told Mr. *Fainall* of your Ladyship then?

MRS FAINALL.   Ay, all's out, My affair with *Mirabell*, every
thing discover'd. This is the last day of our liveing together, that's
my Comfort.   75

FOIBLE.   Indeed *Madam*, and so 'tis a Comfort if you knew all,
——he has been even with your Ladyship; which I cou'd have
told you long enough since, but I love to keep Peace and Quiet-
ness by my good will: I had rather bring friends together, than
set 'em at distance. But Mrs. *Marwood* and He are nearer related   80
than ever their Parents thought for.

MRS FAINALL.   Say'st thou so *Foible*? Canst thou prove this?

FOIBLE.　I can take my Oath of it *Madam*, so can Mrs. *Mincing*;
we have had many a fair word from *Madam Marwood*, to
conceal something that pass'd in our Chamber one Evening when　85
you were at *Hide-Park*;———And we were thought to have gone
a Walking: But we went up unawares,———tho' we were sworn to
secresie too; *Madam Marwood* took a Book and swore us upon
it: But it was but a Book of Verses and Poems,———So as long as
it was not a Bible-Oath, we may break it with a safe Conscience.　90

MRS FAINALL.　This discovery is the most opportune thing I
cou'd wish. Now *Mincing*?

Enter MINCING.

MINCING.　My Lady wou'd speak with Mrs. *Foible*, *Mem*. Mr.
Mirabell is with her, he has set your Spouse at liberty Mrs. *Foible*;
and wou'd have you hide your self in my Lady's Closet, till my　95
old Lady's anger is abated. O, my old Lady is in a perilous
passion, at something Mr. *Fainall* has said. He swears, and my old
Lady cry's. There's a fearful Hurricane I vow. He says *Mem*, how
that he'll have my Lady's Fortune made over to him, or he'll be
divorc'd.　100

MRS FAINALL.　Do's your Lady and *Mirabell* know that?

MINCING.　Yes *Mem*, they have sent me to see if Sir *Wilfull* be
sober, and to bring him to them. My Lady is resolv'd to have him
I think, rather than loose such a vast Summ as six thousand
Pound. O, come Mrs. *Foible*, I hear my old Lady.　105

MRS FAINALL.　*Foible*, you must tell *Mincing*, that she must
prepare to vouch when I call her.

FOIBLE.　Yes, yes *Madam*.

MINCING.　O yes *Mem*, I'll vouch any thing for your Ladyship's
service, be what it will.　110

Exeunt MINCING *and* FOIBLE.

Enter LADY WISHFORT *and* MRS MARWOOD.

LADY WISHFORT.　O my dear Friend, how can I Enumerate
the benefits that I have receiv'd from your goodness? To you I
owe the timely discovery of the false vows of *Mirabell*; To you
the Detection of the Impostor Sir *Rowland*. And now you are
become an Intercessor with my Son in-Law, to save the Honour　115
of my House, and Compound for the frailties of my Daughter.

Well Friend, You are enough to reconcile me to the bad World,
or else I wou'd retire to Desarts and Solitudes; and feed harmless
Sheep by *Groves* and *Purling Streams*. Dear *Marwood*, let us
leave the World, and retire by our selves and be *Shepherdesses*.   120

MRS MARWOOD.   Let us first dispatch the affair in hand *Madam*,
we shall have leisure to think of Retirement afterwards. Here is
one who is concern'd in the treaty.

LADY WISHFORT.   O Daughter, Daughter, Is it possible thou
shoud'st be my Child, Bone of my Bone, and Flesh of my Flesh,   125
and as I may say, another Me, and yet transgress the most minute
Particle of severe Vertue? Is it possible you should lean aside to
Iniquity who have been Cast in the direct Mold of Vertue? I have
not only been a Mold but a Pattern for you, and a Model for you,
after you were brought into the World.   130

MRS FAINALL.   I don't understand your Ladyship.

LADY WISHFORT.   Not understand? Why have you not been
Naught? Have you not been Sophisticated? Not understand?
Here I am ruin'd to Compound for your *Caprices* and your
Cuckoldomes. I must pawn my *Plate*, and my *Jewells* and ruine my   135
Neice, and all little enough——

MRS FAINALL.   I am wrong'd and abus'd, and so are you. 'Tis a
false accusation, as false as *Hell*, as false as your Friend there, ay
or your Friend's Friend, my false Husband.

MRS MARWOOD.   My Friend, Mrs. *Fainal*? Your husband my   140
Friend, what do you mean?

MRS FAINALL.   I know what I mean *Madam*, and so do you;
and so shall the World at a time Convenient.

MRS MARWOOD.   I am sorry to see you so passionate, *Madam*.
More Temper wou'd look more like Innocence. But I have done.   145
I am sorry my Zeal to serve your Ladyship and Family, shou'd
admit of Misconstruction, or make me liable to affronts. You
will pardon me, *Madam*, If I meddle no more with an affair, in
which I am not Personally concern'd.

LADY WISHFORT.   O dear Friend; I am so asham'd that you   150
should meet with such returns;——you ought to ask Pardon on
your Knees, Ungratefull Creature; she deserves more from you,
than all your life can accomplish——O don't leave me destitute
in this Perplexity;——No, stick to me my good Genius.

MRS FAINALL.   I tell you *Madam* you're abus'd——stick to   155

you? ay, like a *Leach*, to suck your best Blood——she'll drop off
when she's full. *Madam* you sha'not pawn a *Bodkin*, nor part with
a *Brass Counter* in Composition for me. I defie 'em all. Let 'em
prove their aspersions: I know my own Innocence, and dare stand
by a tryall.   160

Exit.

LADY WISHFORT. Why, If she shou'd be Innocent, If she
shou'd be wrong'd after all, ha! I don't know what to think,——
and I promise you, her Education has been unexceptionable——
I may say it; for I chiefly made it my own Care to Initiate her very
Infancy in the Rudiments of Vertue, and to Impress upon her   165
tender Years, a Young *Odium* and *Aversion* to the very sight of
Men,——ay Friend, she wou'd ha' shriek'd, If she had but seen
a Man, till she was in her Teens. As I'm a Person 'tis true——
She was never suffer'd to play with a Male-Child, tho' but in
Coats; Nay her very Babies were of the *Feminine Gender*,——O,   170
she never look'd a Man in the Face but her own Father, or the
Chaplain, and him we made a shift to put upon her for a Woman,
by the help of his long Garments, and his Sleek-face; till she was
going in her fifteen.

MRS MARWOOD. Twas much she shou'd be deceiv'd so long.   175

LADY WISHFORT. I warrant you, or she wou'd never have born
to have been Catechis'd by him; and have heard his long lectures,
against Singing and Dancing, and such Debaucheries; and going
to filthy *Plays*; and Profane *Musick-meetings*, where the Leud
Trebles squeek nothing but Bawdy, and the Bases roar *Blas-*   180
phemy. O, she wou'd have swooned at the sight or name of an
obscene Play-Book——and can I think after all this, that my
Daughter can be Naught? What, a Whore? And thought it
excommunication to set her foot within the door of a Play-house.
O my dear friend, I can't believe it, No, no; as she says, let him 185
prove it, let him prove it.

MRS MARWOOD. Prove it *Madam*? What, and have your name
prostituted in a publick Court; Yours and your Daughters
reputation worry'd at the Barr by a pack of Bawling Lawyers?
To be usherd in with an *O Yez* of Scandal; and have your Case   190
open'd by an old fumbling Leacher in a Quoif like a Man Midwife to bring your Daughter's Infamy to light, to be a Theme for

D

legal Punsters, and Quiblers by the Statute; and become a Jest, against a Rule of Court, where there is no precedent for a Jest in any record; not even in *Dooms-day-Book*: to discompose the 195 gravity of the Bench, and provoke Naughty Interrogatories, in more Naughty *Law Latin*; while the good Judge tickl'd with the proceeding, Simpers under a Grey beard, and fidges off and on his Cushion as if he had swallow'd *Cantharides*, or sat upon *Cow-Itch*.

LADY WISHFORT.   O, 'tis very hard!   200

MRS MARWOOD.   And then to have my Young *Revellers* of the *Temple*, take Notes like Prentices at a *Conventicle*; and after, talk it all over again in Commons, or before Drawers in an *Eating-house*.

LADY WISHFORT.   Worse and Worse.   205

MRS MARWOOD.   Nay this is nothing; if it wou'd end here, 'twere well. But it must after this be consign'd by the Short-hand Writers to the publick Press; and from thence be transferr'd to the hands, nay into the Throats and Lungs of Hawkers, with Voices more Licentious than the loud *Flounder-man*'s or the *Woman* 210 that crys *Grey-pease*; and this you must hear till you are stunn'd; Nay you must hear nothing else for some days.

LADY WISHFORT.   O, 'tis Insupportable. No, no, dear Friend make it up, make it up; ay, ay, I'll Compound. I'll give up all, my self and my all, my *Neice* and her all,——any thing, every thing 215 for Composition.

MRS MARWOOD.   Nay *Madam*, I advise nothing, I only lay before you as a Friend the Inconveniencies which perhaps you have Overseen. Here comes Mr. *Fainall*. If he will be satisfi'd to huddle up all in Silence, I shall be glad. You must think I would 220 rather Congratulate, than Condole with you.

Enter FAINALL.

LADY WISHFORT.   Ay, ay, I do not doubt it, dear *Marwood*: No, no, I do not doubt it.

FAINALL.   Well Madam; I have suffer'd my self to be overcome by the Importunity of this Lady your Friend; and am content you 225 shall enjoy your own proper Estate during Life; on condition you oblige your self never to Marry, under such penalty as I think convenient.

LADY WISHFORT.   Never to Marry?

FAINALL.   No more Sir *Rowlands*,——the next Imposture may   230
not be so timely detected.

MRS MARWOOD.   That condition I dare answer, my Lady will
consent to, without difficulty; she has already, but too much
experienc'd the perfidiousness of Men. Besides Madam, when we
retire to our pastoral Solitude we shall bid adieu to all other   235
Thoughts.

LADY WISHFORT.   Aye that's true; but in Case of Necessity;
as of Health, or some such Emergency——

FAINALL.   O, if you are prescrib'd Marriage, you shall be consider'd; I will only reserve to my self the Power to chuse for you.   240
If your Physick be wholsome, it matters not who is your Apothe-
cary. Next, my Wife shall settle on me the remainder of her Fortune, not made over already; And for her Maintenance depend
entirely on my Discretion.

LADY WISHFORT.   This is most inhumanly Savage; exceeding   245
the Barbarity of a *Muscovite* Husband.

FAINALL.   I learn'd it from his *Czarish* Majestie's Retinue, in a
Winter Evenings Conference over Brandy and Pepper, amongst
other secrets of Matrimony and Policy, as they are at present
Practis'd in the *Northern* Hemisphere. But this must be agreed   250
unto, and that positively. Lastly, I will be endow'd in right of my
Wife, with that six thousand Pound, which is the Moiety of Mrs.
Millamant's Fortune in your Possession: And which she has
forfeited (as will appear by the last Will and Testament of your
deceas'd Husband Sir *Jonathan Wishfort*) by her disobedience in   255
Contracting her self against your Consent or Knowledge; and by
refusing the offer'd Match with Sir *Willfull Witwou'd*, which you
like a careful Aunt had provided for her.

LADY WISHFORT.   My Nephew was *non Compos*; and cou'd
not make his Addresses.   260

FAINALL.   I come to make demands,——I'll hear no objections.

LADY WISHFORT.   You will grant me time to Consider.

FAINALL.   Yes, while the Instrument is drawing, to which you
must set your Hand till more sufficient Deeds can be perfected,
which I will take care shall be done with all possible speed. In the   265
mean while, I will go for the said Instrument, and till my return,
you may Ballance this Matter in your own Discretion.

                                    Exit FAINALL.

LADY WISHFORT.   This Insolence is beyond all Precedent, all
   Parallel, must I be subject to this merciless Villain?

MRS MARWOOD.   'Tis severe indeed *Madam*, that you shou'd   270
   smart for your Daughters wantonness.

LADY WISHFORT.   'Twas against my Consent that she Married
   this Barbarian, But she wou'd have him, tho' her Year was not
   out.——Ah! her first Husband my Son *Languish*, would not have
   carry'd it thus. Well, that was my Choice, this is her's; she is   275
   match'd now with a Witness——I shall be mad, Dear Friend, is
   there no Comfort for me? Must I live to be confiscated at this
   Rebel-rate?——Here come two more of my *Egyptian* Plagues
   too.

Enter MILLAMANT *and* SIR WILFULL.

SIR WILFULL.   Aunt, your Servant.   280

LADY WISHFORT.   Out *Caterpillar*, Call not me Aunt, I know
   thee not.

SIR WILFULL.   I confess I have been a little in disguise as they
   say,——S'heart! and I'm sorry for't. What wou'd you have? I
   hope I committed no Offence Aunt——and if I did I am willing   285
   to make satisfaction; and what can a man say fairer? If I have
   broke any thing, I'll pay for't, an it cost a Pound. And so let that
   content for what's past, and make no more words. For what's to
   come to pleasure you I'm willing to marry my Cosen. So pray
   lets all be Friends, she and I are agreed upon the matter, before a   290
   Witness.

LADY WISHFORT.   How's this dear *Niece*? Have I any comfort?
   Can this be true?

MILLAMANT.   I am content to be a Sacrifice to your repose
   Madam; and to Convince you that I had no hand in the Plot, as   295
   you were misinform'd; I have laid my commands on *Mirabell* to
   come in Person, and be a Witness that I gave my hand to this
   flower of *Knight-hood*; and for the Contract that past between
   Mirabell and me, I have oblig'd him to make a Resignation of it,
   in your Lady-ship's presence;——He is without and waits your   300
   leave for admittance.

LADY WISHFORT.   Well, I'll swear I am something reviv'd at
   this Testimony of your Obedience; but I cannot admit that
   Traytor,——I fear I cannot fortifie my self to support his appear-

ance. He is as terrible to me as a *Gorgon*; if I see him, I fear I shall   305
turn to Stone, petrifie Incessantly.

MILLAMANT.   If you disoblige him he may resent your refusal
and insist upon the contract still. Then 'tis the last time he will be
offensive to you.

LADY WISHFORT.   Are you sure it will be the last time?——   310
if I were sure of that——shall I never see him again?

MILLAMANT.   Sir *Willfull*, you and he are to Travel together,
are you not?

SIR WILFULL.   'Sheart the Gentleman's a civil Gentleman, Aunt,
let him come in; why we are sworn Brothers and fellow Travel-   315
lers.——We are to be *Pylades* and *Orestes*, he and I——He is
to be my Interpreter in foreign Parts. He has been Over-sea's
once already; and with proviso that I Marry my Cosen, will
cross 'em once again, only to bear me Company,——'Sheart,
I'll call him in,——an I set on't once, he shall come in; and see   320
who'll hinder him.

Exit.

MRS MARWOOD.   This is precious Fooling, if it wou'd pass, but
I'll know the bottom of it.

LADY WISHFORT.   O dear *Marwood*, you are not going?

MRS MARWOOD.   Not far *Madam*; I'll return immediately.   325

Exit.

Re-enter SIR WILFULL *and* MIRABELL.

SIR WILFULL.   Look up Man, I'll stand by you, 'sbud an she do
frown, she can't kill you;——besides——Hearkee she dare not
frown desperately, because her face is none of her own; 'Sheart
an she shou'd her forehead wou'd wrinkle like the Coat of a
Cream-cheese, but mum for that, fellow Traveller.   330

MIRABELL.   If a deep sense of the many Injuries I have offer'd to
so good a Lady, with a sincere remorse, and a hearty Contrition,
can but obtain the least glance of Compassion I am too Happy,
——Ah *Madam*, there was a time——but let it be forgotten
——I confess I have deservedly forfeited the high Place I once   335
held, of sighing at your Feet; nay kill me not, by turning from me
in disdain,——I come not to plead for favour;——Nay not for
Pardon, I am a Suppliant only for your pity——I am going where
I never shall behold you more——

SIR WILFULL.   How, fellow Traveller!——You shall go by 340
your self then.

MIRABELL.   Let me be pitied first; and afterwards forgotten,——
I ask no more.

SIR WILFULL.   By'r Lady a very reasonable request; and will
cost you nothing, Aunt——Come, come, Forgive and Forget 345
Aunt, why you must an you are a Christian.

MIRABELL.   Consider *Madam*, in reality; You cou'd not receive
much prejudice; it was an Innocent device; tho' I confess it had
a face of guiltiness,——it was at most an Artifice which Love
Contriv'd——and errours which Love produces have ever been 350
accounted *Venial*. At least think it is Punishment enough, that
I have lost what in my heart I hold most dear, that to your cruel
Indignation, I have offer'd up this Beauty, and with her my
Peace and Quiet; Nay all my hopes of future Comfort.

SIR WILFULL.   An he do's not move me, wou'd I might never be 355
O' the Quorum——an it were not as good a deed as to drink, to
give her to him again,——I wou'd I might never take Shipp-
ing——Aunt, if you don't forgive quickly; I shall melt, I can
tell you that. My contract went no further than a little Mouth-
Glew, and that's hardly dry;——One dolefull Sigh more from 360
my fellow Traveller and 'tis dissolv'd.

LADY WISHFORT.   Well *Nephew*, upon your account——ah,
he has a false Insinuating Tongue——Well Sir, I will stifle my
just resentment at my *Nephew's* request.——I will endeavour
what I can to forget,——but on *proviso* that you resign 365
the Contract with my *Neice* Immediately.

MIRABELL.   It is in Writing and with Papers of Concern; but I
have sent my Servant for it, and will deliver it to you, with all
acknowledgments for your transcendent goodness.

LADY WISHFORT.   [*Apart.*] Oh, he has *Witch-craft* in his Eyes 370
and Tongue;——When I did not see him I cou'd have brib'd a
Villain to his Assassination; but his appearance rakes the *Embers*
which have so long layn smother'd in my Breast.——

Enter FAINALL *and* MRS MARWOOD.

FAINALL.   Your date of deliberation *Madam*, is expir'd. Here is
the Instrument, are you prepar'd to sign? 375

LADY WISHFORT.   If I were prepar'd; I am not Impowr'd. My

Neice exerts a lawfull claim, having Match'd her self by my direction to Sir *Wilfull*.

FAINALL.   That sham is too gross to pass on me,——tho 'tis Impos'd on you, *Madam*.   380

MILLAMANT.   Sir, I have given my consent.

MIRABELL.   And Sir, I have resign'd my pretensions.

SIR WILFULL.   And Sir, I assert my right; and will maintain it in defiance of you Sir, and of your Instrument. S'heart an you talk of an Instrument Sir, I have an old *Fox* by my Thigh shall   385 hack your Instrument of *Ram Vellam* to shreds, Sir. It shall not be sufficient for a *Mittimus* or a *Taylor's* measure; therefore withdraw your Instrument Sir, or by'r Lady I shall draw mine.

LADY WISHFORT.   Hold *Nephew*, hold.

MILLAMANT.   Good Sir *Wilfull* respite your valour.   390

FAINALL.   Indeed? are you provided of a Guard, with your single Beef-eater there? but I'm prepar'd for you; and Insist upon my first proposal. You shall submit your own Estate to my management, And absolutely make over my Wife's to my sole use; As pursuant to the Purport and Tenor of this other Covenant,   395 ——I suppose *Madam*, your Consent is not requisite in this Case; nor Mr. *Mirabell*, your resignation; nor Sir *Wilfull*, your right——You may draw your *Fox* if you please Sir, and make a *Bear-Garden* flourish somewhere else; For here it will not avail. This, my Lady *Wishfor't*, must be subscrib'd, or your Darling   400 Daughter's turn'd a drift, like a Leaky hulk to Sink or Swim, as she and the Current of this Lewd Town can agree.

LADY WISHFORT.   Is there no means, no Remedy, to stop my ruine? Ungrateful Wretch! dost thou not owe thy being, thy subsistance to my Daughter's Fortune?   405

FAINALL.   I'll answer you when I have the rest of it in my possession.

MIRABELL.   But that you wou'd not accept of a Remedy from my hands——I own I have not deserv'd you shou'd owe any Obligation to me; or else perhaps I cou'd advise.——   410

LADY WISHFORT.   O what? what? to save me and my Child from Ruine, from Want, I'll forgive all that's past; Nay I'll consent to any thing to come, to be deliver'd from this Tyranny.

MIRABELL.   Ay *Madam*; but that is too late, my reward is intercepted. You have dispos'd of her, who only cou'd have made me   415

a Compensation for all my Services;——But be it as it may. I am
resolv'd I'll serve you, you shall not be wrong'd in this *Savage*
manner.

LADY WISHFORT.   How! dear Mr. *Mirabell*, can you be so
generous at last! But it is not possible. *Hearkee*, I'll break my   420
Nephews Match, you shall have my *Niece* yet, and all her fortune;
if you can but save me from this imminent danger.

MIRABELL.   Will you? I take you at your word. I ask no more. I
must have leave for two Criminals to appear.

LADY WISHFORT.   Ay, ay, any Body, any body.   425

MIRABELL.   *Foible* is one and a Penitent.

Enter MRS FAINALL, FOIBLE, *and* MINCING.

MRS MARWOOD.   O my shame!

> MIRABELL *and* LADY WISHFORT *go to* MRS FAINALL,
> ⟨MINCING,⟩ *and* FOIBLE.

These Corrupt things are bought and brought hither to expose
me——[*to* FAINALL.]

FAINALL.   If it must all come out, why let 'em know it, 'tis but   430
the way of the World. That shall not urge me to relinquish or abate
one tittle of my Terms, no, I will insist the more.

FOIBLE.   Yes indeed *Madam*; I'll take my Bible-oath of it.

MINCING.   And so will I, *Mem*.

LADY WISHFORT.   O *Marwood*, *Marwood* art thou false? my   435
friend deceive me? hast thou been a wicked accomplice with that
profligate man?

MRS MARWOOD.   Have you so much Ingratitude and Injustice,
to give credit against your Friend, to the Aspersions of two such
Mercenary Truls?   440

MINCING.   Mercenary, *Mem*? I scorn your words. 'Tis true we
found you and Mr. *Fainall* in the Blew garret; by the same token,
you swore us to Secresie upon *Messalinas*'s Poems. Mercenary?
No, if we wou'd have been Mercenary, we shou'd have held our
Tongues; You wou'd have brib'd us sufficiently.   445

FAINALL.   Go, you are an Insignificant thing,——Well, what
are you the better for this? Is this Mr. *Mirabell*'s Expedient? I'll
be put off no longer——You thing that was a Wife, shall smart

for this. I will not leave thee wherewithall to hide thy Shame; Your Body shall be Naked as your Reputation.   450

MRS FAINALL.   I despise you and defie your Malice——You have aspers'd me wrongfully——I have prov'd your falsehood ——Go you and your treacherous——I will not name it, but starve together——perish.

FAINALL.   Not while you are worth a Groat, indeed my dear   455 *Madam*, I'll be fool'd no longer.

LADY WISHFORT. Ah Mr. *Mirabell*, this is small comfort, the detection of this affair.

MIRABELL.   O in good time——Your leave for the other Offender and Penitent to appear, *Madam*.   460

Enter WAITWELL *with a Box of Writings.*

LADY WISHFORT.   O Sir *Rowland*——well Rascal.

WAITWELL.   What your Ladyship pleases.——I have brought the Black box at last, *Madam*.

MIRABELL.   Give it me. *Madam*, you remember your promise.

LADY WISHFORT.   I, dear Sir!   465

MIRABELL.   Where are the Gentlemen?

WAITWELL.   At hand Sir, rubbing their Eyes,——Just risen from Sleep.

FAINALL.   S'death what's this to me? I'll not wait your private concerns.   470

Enter PETULANT *and* WITWOUD.

PETULANT.   How now? what's the matter? who's hand's out?

WITWOUD.   Hey day! what are you all got together like Players at the end of the last Act?

MIRABELL.   You may remember Gentlemen, I once requested your hands as Witnesses to a certain Parchment.   475

WITWOUD.   Ay I do, my hand I remember——*Petulant* set his Mark.

MIRABELL.   You wrong him, his name is fairly written as shall appear——you do not remember Gentlemen, any thing of what that Parchment contain'd——   480

Undoing the Box.

WITWOUD.   No.

E

PETULANT. Not I. I writ. I read nothing.

MIRABELL. Very well, now you shall know——*Madam*, your promise.

LADY WISHFORT. Ay, ay, Sir, upon my honour. 485

MIRABELL. Mr. *Fainall*, it is now time that you shou'd know, that your Lady while she was at her own disposal, and before you had by your Insinuations wheadl'd her out of a pretended Settlement of the greatest part of her fortune——

FAINALL. Sir! pretended! 490

MIRABELL. Yes Sir. I say that this Lady while a Widdow, having it seems receiv'd some Cautions respecting your Inconstancy and Tyranny of temper, which from her own partial Opinion and fondness of you, she cou'd never have suspected——she did I say by the wholesome advice of Friends and of Sages learned in 495 the Laws of this Land, deliver this same as her Act and Deed to me in trust, and to the uses within mention'd. You may read if you please——[*holding out the Parchment*] tho perhaps what is inscrib'd on the back may serve your occasions.

FAINALL. Very likely Sir, What's here? Damnation! [*Reads.*] 500 *A deed of Conveyance of the whole Estate real of* Arabella Languish *Widdow in trust to* Edward Mirabell.
Confusion!

MIRABELL. Even so Sir, 'tis *the way of the World*, Sir: of the Widdows of the World. I suppose this Deed may bear an Elder 505 Date than what you have obtain'd from your Lady.

FAINALL. Perfidious Fiend! then thus I'll be reveng'd.

Offers to run at MRS FAINALL.

SIR WILFULL. Hold Sir, now you may make your *Bear-Garden* flourish somewhere else Sir.

FAINALL. *Mirabell*, You shall hear of this Sir, be sure you shall, 510 let me pass *Oafe*.

Exit.

MRS FAINALL. *Madam*, you seem to stifle your Resentment: You have better give it Vent.

MRS MARWOOD. Yes it shall have Vent——and to your Confusion, or I'll perish in the attempt. 515

Exit.

LADY WISHFORT. O Daughter, Daughter, 'tis plain thou hast inherited thy Mother's prudence.

MRS FAINALL. Thank Mr. *Mirabell*, a Cautious Friend, to whose advice all is owing.

LADY WISHFORT. Well Mr. *Mirabell*, you have kept your promise,——and I must perform mine.——First I pardon for your sake, Sir *Rowland* there and *Foible*,——The next thing is to break the Matter to my *Nephew*——and how to do that—— 520

MIRABELL. For that *Madam*, give your self no trouble——let me have your Consent——Sir *Wilfull* is my Friend; he has had compassion upon Lovers and generously engag'd a Volunteer in this Action, for our Service, and now designs to prosecute his Travells. 525

SIR WILFULL. S'heart Aunt, I have no mind to marry. My Cosen's a Fine Lady, and the Gentleman loves her and she loves him, and they deserve one another; my resolution is to see Foreign Parts——I have set on't——And when I'm set on't, I must do't. And if these two Gentlemen wou'd Travel too, I think they may be spar'd. 530

PETULANT. For my part, I say little——I think things are best off or on. 535

WITWOUD. I Gad I understand nothing of the matter,——I'm in a maze yet, like a *Dog* in a *Dancing School*.

LADY WISHFORT. Well Sir, take her, and with her all the Joy I can give you. 540

MILLAMANT. Why do's not the man take me? wou'd you have me give my self to you over again.

MIRABELL. Ay, and over and over again; [*kisses her hand*] for I wou'd have you as often as possibly I can. Well, heav'n grant I love you not too well, that's all my fear. 545

SIR WILFULL. S'heart you'll have him time enough to toy after you're married; or if you will toy now, let us have a Dance in the mean time, that we who are not Lovers, may have some other employment, besides looking on.

MIRABELL. With all my heart dear Sir *Willfull*, what shall we do for Musick? 550

FOIBLE. O Sir, Some that were provided for Sir *Rowland*'s Entertainment are yet within Call.

A Dance.

LADY WISHFORT.   As I am a person I can hold out no longer;
——I have wasted my spirits so to day already; that I am ready   555
to sink under the fatigue; and I cannot but have some fears
upon me yet, that my Son *Fainall* will pursue some desperate
Course.

MIRABELL.   *Madam*, disquiet not your self on that account, to
my knowledge his Circumstances are such, he must of force
comply. For my part I will Contribute all that in me lies to a Re-   560
union: In the mean time, *Madam*, [*to* MRS FAINALL] let me
before these Witnesses, restore to you this deed of trust. It may
be a means well manag'd to make you live Easily together.

> *From hence let those be warn'd, who mean to wed;*
> *Lest mutual falshood stain the Bridal-Bed:*   565
> *For each deceiver to his cost may find,*
> *That marriage frauds too oft are paid in kind.*

Exeunt Omnes.

EPILOGUE.

Spoken by Mrs. *Bracegirdle*.

After our *Epilogue* this Crowd dismisses,
I'm thinking how this Play'll be pull'd to Pieces.
But pray consider, ere you doom its fall,
How hard a thing 'twould be, to please you all.
There are some Criticks so with Spleen diseas'd,   5
They scarcely come inclining to be Pleas'd:
And sure he must have more than mortal Skill,
Who pleases any one against his Will.
Then, all bad Poets we are sure are Foes,
And how their Number's swell'd the Town well knows: 10
In shoals, I've mark'd 'em judging in the Pit;
Tho' they're on no pretence for Judgment fit
But that they have been Damn'd for want of wit.
Since when, they by their own offences taught
Set up for Spys on Plays and finding Fault.   15

Others there are whose Malice we'd prevent; ⎫
Such, who watch Plays, with scurrilous intent ⎬
To mark out who by *Characters* are meant. ⎭
And tho' no perfect likeness they can Trace;
Yet each pretends to know the *Copy'd Face*.   20
These with false Glosses, feed their own Ill-nature,
And turn to *Libel*, what was meant a *Satire*.
May such malicious *Fops* this Fortune find,
To think themselves alone the *Fools* design'd:
If any are so arrogantly Vain, ⎫   25
To think they *singly* can support a *Scene*, ⎬
And furnish *Fool* enough to entertain. ⎭
For well the Learn'd and the Judicious know, ⎫
That *Satire* scorns to stoop so meanly low, ⎬
As any *one abstracted Fop* to shew. ⎭   30
For, as when Painters form a matchless Face,
They from each *Fair One* catch some different Grace;
And shining Features in one Portrait blend,
To which no single Beauty must pretend:
So Poets oft, do in one Piece expose   35
Whole *Belles Assemblées* of *Cocquetts* and *Beaux*.

TEXTUAL NOTES

SIGLA

Q1	=	First Quarto, 1700; Q1^u = First Quarto, uncorrected; Q1^c = First Quarto, corrected.
Q2	=	Second Quarto, 1706.
W1	=	Works, 1710.
W2	=	Works, 1719.
BATESON	=	*The Works of Congreve*, ed. F. W. Bateson. London (Peter Davies); New York (Minton, Balch & Co.) 1930.
DAVIS	=	*The Complete Plays of William Congreve*, ed. H. J. Davis. Chicago and London (University of Chicago Press) 1966.

DED.

25 ridiculous] Q1; ridicul'd Q2, W1–2.
54 Laugh out] Q1; laugh at W1–2.
59 He$_\wedge$] Q2;~, Q1.
82 equal to the Capacity of] Q1; equal in Capacity to W1–2.

PER. DRAM.

PERSONÆ DRAMATIS] Q1;
   DRAMATIS PERSONAE W1–2.
MEN. By] Q1; MEN. Q2, W1–2.
WOMEN. By] Q1^c; WOMEN. Q1^u, Q2, W1–2.

I. I

73 that] Q1; this Q2, W1–2.
76 without] Q1; unless W1–2.

89 confesses] Q1; confesses that W2.
90 than your] Q1; than is your W1–2.
99 S.D. SERVANT] Q1; FOOTMAN W1–2. W1 *and* W2 *do not, however, change subsequent speech-headings to match.*
104 besides] Q2; Besides Q1.
117 Pond; that] Q2; ~ . That Q1.
130 that is] Q1; who is one W1–2.
167 *Witwoud?*] Q1; ~ ! W2.
196 the t'other] Q1; t'other W1–2.
213 the]Q1; a W1–2.
213 one$_\wedge$but now,] Q2; ~ , ~ ~ $_\wedge$Q1.
232 But she's] Q1; she's W2.
236 Judgment$_\wedge$*Mirabell*.] Q1; ~ , ~ ? W1–2.
258–9 honest Fellow, and a very pretty] Q1; pretty Fellow, and a very honest W2.
261 him neither$_\wedge$] Q1; ~ ~ . Q2; him. W1–2.

262 had but any] Q1; had any w1–2.
263 Come,] Q2; ~ ‸ Q1.
268 Pity faith] Q1; pity w1–2.
283 Friend.] Q1; ~ ! w2.
310 the] Q1; a w1–2.
315 s.d. BETTY *and* COACHMAN] w1–2
     make it clear that both characters
     leave.
322 that] Q1; whom w1–2.
331 Mean,] Q1; ~ ! w2.
334 and Mask] Q1; and a Mask w1–2.
335 trice;] Q1; ~ ! w2.
341 s.d. *and* BETTY] w1–2 *make it clear*
     that Betty enters.
353 Condition,] Q1; ~ ! w2.
364 I;] Q1; ~ ? w2. w2's *reading is*
     clearer than Q1's.
367 that] Q1; who w1–2.
369 he] Q1; he had w1–2.
373 me, dear] Q1; ~ . Dear w2.
387 nothing.—] Q2; ~ - — Q1.
392 Explain,] Q1; ~ ; w1; ~ ! w2.
404 I,] Q1; ~ ? w2.
441 Parrot, or than] Q2; Parrot: Or
     then Q1.
457 Do you.] Q1; You do? w1–2.
474 a Fire] Q1; Fire w1–2.

II. 1

 7 as such fly] Q1; as from such, fly
     w1–2.
 18 with] Q1; to w1–2.
 32 Mankind?] w1; ~ . Q1–2.
 34 Husband?] w1; ~ . Q1–2.
 58 Why,] Q1; ~ ‸ Q2, w1.
127 I do now] Q1; I do not now Q2,
     w1–2. *Apparently* not *is an over-*
     sight in Q2ff.
143 slept!] Q1; ~ ? w2.
145 loving of another] Q1; loving
     another w1–2.
150 Instance?] Q1; ~ ! w1–2.
158 then!] Q1; ~ ? w1–2.
173 Competition] Q2; Competion Q1.
234 I've] Q1 ; I have Q2.

236 we'll] w1; will Q1–2.
237 any where,] w1; ~ ~ ‸ Q1–2.
237 World,] Q1; ~ . w2.
238 Sdeath‸] Q1; ~ ! w2.
255–6 apprehensive] Q2; aprehensive
     Q1.
286 Condition she] Q1; Condition that
     she w1–2.
294 a] Q1; an w1–2.
309 her Streamers] Q1; Streamers w1–2.
320 in disgrace] Q1; just disgraced
     w1–2.
342 Pecquet] Q1; Pacquet Q2, w1–2.
     Bateson (p. 503) *ascribes* Q2's *error*
     to a compositorial misunderstanding
     of Mincing's idiom.
351–2 I fancy ... with Prose.] Q1;
     omitted Q2, w1–2.
355 Cremp] Q1; Cramp Q2, w1–2. Cf.
     note on l. 374 above.
361 Did not] Q1; Did w1–2.
374 vain,] Q2; ~ ‸ Q1.
375 be!] Q1; ~ ? w1–2.
404 Fiction;] Q1; ~ ! w2.
421 than] Q2; then Q1.
448 one] Q1; a w1–2.
454 woo] Q2; woe Q1.
458 that *Foible's*] Q1; *Foible's* Q2, w1–2.
461 Unless by] Q1; Without w1–2.
464 that,] Q2; ~ ; Q1.
528 I am] Q1; I'm Q2, w1–2.
530 *the Grief*] Q1; *my Grief* Q2, w1–2.

III. 1

11–12 *Ratifia‸ Fool*—] Q1; ~ , ~ —
     Q2, w1; ~ , ~ ? w2.
 14 thee.] Q1; ~ ? w1–2.
 17 I cannot] Q1; cannot w1–2.
 21 Cherry–] Q2; Chery– Q1.
 32 What,] w1; ~ ‸ Q1–2.
 35 *Maritornes*] w1; *Maritorne's* Q1–2.
 41 *dishabilie*] Q1; *dishabillé* Q2, w1–2.
 58 Go you Thing and send her in.]
     Q1; *moved to follow l.63 in* w1 *and*
     w2, *the end of Scene* IV.

69 Well, here it is . . . kiss'd away—]
Q1; *omitted* Q2, W1–2.

99 Villain,] Q1; ~ ! W2.

116 Hands] Q1; Hand Q2, W1–2.

117 Frippery?] Q1; ~ ! Q2, W1–2.

120 Long-Lane] Q2; long Lane Q1.

120 slander-mouth'd] Q2; ~ ₍ ~ Q1.

142 a] Q1; he W2.

154 swimminess] Q1; swimmingness
Q2, W1–2.

163 Nothing but . . . Decorums] Q1;
omitted Q2, W1–2.

198 S.D. *Enter* FOOTMAN.] Q1; *Calls.*
W1–2.

205 *Pass-par-tout*] Q1; *Pass-par-toute*
W1–2.

206 Bodies] Q1; Body's Q2, W1–2.

219–20 and stalk . . . at a Fortune]
Q1; *omitted* W1–2.

251 dress'd] Q2; dressld Q1.

259 into] Q2; into into Q1.

267 I'll] Q1; I Q2, W1–2.

270 the] Q1; that W1–2.

279 glossy] Q1; glosly Q2, W1.

279 Fool₍] Q2; ~ , Q1.

295 dressing] Q1; dressing here W1–2.

296 Mallice. *Exit* MINCING. The Town
. . . it.] Malice. The . . . it. (*Exit*
Mincing.) Q2; ~ , the . . . it. (*Exit*
Mincing.) Q1; *in* W1–2 Mallice.
is followed by the heading for Scene
XI—i.e., *Mincing exits after Mal-*
lice. not after the next sentence as in
Q1–2. *The changes in* W1–2 *show that*
Millamant's response, The Town
has found it, picks up Mrs Mar-
wood's use of the same words at
l.286, and leads into the next ques-
tion. The reading adopted follows the
punctuation of Q2ff., *which makes*
sense, while the placing of the s.d.
follows W1–2 *for the sake of clarity.*

320 both,] Q1; ~ ₍ Q2, W1–2.

320 think it] Q1; think W2.

326 Ha, ha, ha.] Q1; ha, ha. W2.

331 Melancholly] Q1; melancholick
W1–2.

341 S.D. *and sung by Mrs.* Hodgson]
Q1; *omitted* W1–2.

355 have] Q2; have have Q1.

361 contradict.] Q1; ~ — W1–2.

388 ever the] Q1; any W1–2.

389 Read, any more than] Q1; read,
than W1–2.

401 S.D. *Country Riding Habit . . .*
SERVANT] Q1; *riding Dress . . .*
FOOTMAN W1–2. W1–2 *adopt*
FOOTMAN *throughout the scene.*

409 Sir, yes] Q1; ~ ? ~ W2.

411 here] Q1; hither W1–2.

412 ha!] Q1; ~ ? W1–2.

413 any Body in] Q1; any in W2.

416 Friend?] Q1; ~ ! W1–2.

426 here] Q1; BATESON *emends to*
there, *but cf. the use of* Here . . .
here *at* IV. I. 116.

442 ha, to] Q1; ~ ! To W2.

446 Offence,] Q1; ~ ! W2.

446 Sir] Q2; ~ , Q1.

492 broader] Q1; bigger W1–2.

504 was] Q1; was but W1–2.

506–7 that, Man,] W2; ~ ₍ ~ ₍ Q1–2,
W1. *Although* Q1ff. *make sense,*
W2 *is better in the dramatic con-*
text.

533 Here is] Q1; Here's W1–2.

558 I come] Q1; I am come W2.

566 walk? *Marwood?*] W1; ~ . ~ —
Q1–2.

572 'S death₍] Q1; ~ ! W2.

572 an Anticipated Cuckold] Q1; a
Cuckold by Anticipation W1–2.

574 'S death₍] Q1; ~ ! W2.

577 and out-strip'd] Q1; and be out-
strip'd Q2, W1–2.

593–4 She might throw . . . in her
Pocket] Q1; *omitted* W1–2.

601 reputation, take] Q1; ~ . Take
W1–2.

605 warm,] Q1; ~ ; W1–2.

640 truth—] Q1; ~ , W1–2.

649–50 *Mirabell,* now₍] Q2; ~ . ~ ₍
Q1; ~ ₍ ~ : W1–2.

650 Jealous.] Q1; ~ ? W1–2.

IV. I

24 Room, there's] Q1; ∼ . There's
    w2.
36 in to] w1; into Q1–2.
68 would have] Q1; will ∼ Q2, w1–2.
109 fought] Q1; sought DAVIS, BATE-
    SON. *But no emendation, on the
    grounds that the compositor mistook
    a long "s" for "f", is necessary* (cf.
    Commentary).
133 , when you're dispos'd] Q1; *omit-
    ted* w2.
137 I think...lock'd.] Q1; *unlike* Q1 *later
    editions do not place this sentence on
    a separate line with indentation.*
    Q1's *arrangement may follow an
    attempt in the copy to indicate the
    gap in the sequence of action on the
    stage between Sir Wilfull's final
    compliments and his surprised dis-
    covery that the door is locked.*
147 further. —] Q1; ∼ ? w1–2.
187 Sir] Q2; Sr. Q1.
189 never to be] Q1; never be w1–2.
191 for ever] Q1; ever Q2, w1–2.
199 part. To] Q1; ∼ ; to Q2, w1–2.
233 Gentlewoman] Q1; Gentlewomen
    Q2.
236 Breeding∧ —] w1; ∼ . — Q1–2.
243 me the Father] Q1; me Father
    w1–2.
248 Fashions,] Q2; ∼ ∧ Q1.
251 which,] Q2; ∼ ; Q1.
275 and don't] Q1; don't w1–2.
290 they] Q1; they may w1–2.
294 seems, when] Q1; ∼ ; for w1–2.
304 their] Q1; the w1–2.
306 dispute, they] Q1; ∼ . They w1–2.
309 *Petulant,* ... well;] Q1; ∼ ? ...
    ∼ ? w1–2.
316 *Lacedemonian,* Sirrah∧] Q1; ∼ . ∼ ,
    w1–2.
325 dost] Q2; dodst Q1.
340 then?...it.] Q1; ∼ ;...∼ ? w1–2.
343 wrap] Q2; rap Q1.
352 upon't, at] Q1; ∼ ! ∼ w2.

353 rate.] Q1; ∼ ! w2.
364 *laugh*] Q1; laughs Q2.
370 But] Q2; but Q1.
387 The] Q2; the Q1.
392 do't.] Q2; ∼ , Q1.
400 get thee gone,] Q1; get thee gone,
    get thee gone, w2.
404 *Turks,* no] Q1; ∼ ! ∼ w2.
411 *Diversion,*] Q1; ∼ . w1.
412 and] Q1; or w1–2.
419 s.d. *Enter* FOIBLE ...] Q1; Foible
    whispers Lady W. w1–2. (*In* w1–2
    Foible apparently enters after l.397
    *and so is present throughout Lady
    Wishfort's interview with Sir Wil-
    full.*)
423 Wenches.] Q1; Wenches with
    Broom-sticks. w1–2.
429 him.] Q1; ∼ , Q2, w1–2.
449 a] Q1; the Q2, w1–2.
455 fail,] Q2; ∼ . Q1.
470 Heart-heavings∧] Q2; ∼ , Q1. *The
    punctuation of* Q1 *destroys the
    balance of the sequence of paired
    nouns and verbal nouns.*
480 Well, Sir] Q2; WellSir Q1.
508 undergone;] Q1; ∼ ! w2.
513 iteration] w1; interation Q1–2.
    *It is possible that the misspelling in
    both quartos represents Waitwell's
    ignorant attempt to repeat Lady
    Wishfort's use of the word,* l.486.
522 see by the Superscription it is like]
    Q1; see, the Superscription is like
    w1–2.
524 *Marwood's,*] Q1; ∼ . w2.
530 make you a] Q1; make a w1–2.
539 [*reading*]] BATESON; reading Q1;
    reading, Q2, w1–2.
541 villany! O] Q1; Villany! O Q2; ∼ ∧ O
    Q1.
542 I shall faint, I shall die, I shall die,
    oh!] Q1; I shall faint, I shall die,
    oh! Q2, w1–2.
571 Law?] Q1; ∼ ! Q2, w1–2.
575 face;] Face; Q2; ∼ ∧ Q1.
592 Widdow.] Q1; ∼ : w1–2.

v. 1

6 Traver's] Q1; Traverse w2.

17 the *Merchandize*] the Merchandize w1; your *Merchandize* Q1–2. BATESON *adopts* w *reading. The* Q1–2 *reading is probably a compositorial substitution, by analogy with "your* Commodity" *of the preceding line.*

18 self,] Q2; ~ ∧ Q1.

20 you? Now ... Nest.] Q1; ~ , now ... ~ ? w1–2.

33 damage?] Q1; ~ ! w2.

35 hear] Q2; here Q1.

39 Lady-ship,] Ladiship, Q2; ~ ; Q1.

47 you,] Q1; ~ . Q2, w1–2.

50 be] Q1; be a w2.

59 him, this] Q1; ~ . This w1–2.

68 Confederacy?] Q1; ~ : w2.

89 of Verses and Poems] Q1; of Poems w1–2.

89 So as long as] Q1; so long as Q2, w1–2.

94 her,] Q1; ~ ; Q2, w1–2.

94 liberty∧ Mrs. *Foible*;] Q1; ~ , ~ ~ , Q2, w1–2.

97 said.] DAVIS; ~ , Q1–2; ~ ; w1–2.

98 *Mem*,] w1; ~ ; Q1–2.

101 and] Q1; or w1–2.

104 loose] Q1; lose Q2, w1–2. *It is likely that* "loose" *is a misprint for* "lose"; *however,* Q1 *reading is retained as the sense* "let loose" *is possible here.*

113–4 To you the] Q1; to you I owe the w1–2.

116 frailties] Q2; frailty's Q1.

120 *Shepherdesses*] Q2; *Sheperdresses* Q1.

121–2 *Madam*, we] Q1; ~ . We w1–2.

141 Friend,] Q1; ~ ! w2.

159–60 stand by] Q1; stand w1–2. DAVIS *follows* w1–2.

185 O my dear] Q1; O dear w1–2.

198 fidges] Q1; figes w2. w2's *reading is a possible one, cf.* O.E.D. "fig" (v. 3) *which has the same meaning as* "fidge".

199 sat] Q1; sate Q2, w1–2.

203 all over] Q1; over w1–2.

210–11 *Flounder-man*'s or the *Woman* that crys *Grey-pease*;] Q1; Flounder-man's: w1–2.

219 *Fainall.* If] Q1; ~ , if w1–2.

221 than] Q2; then Q1.

262 Consider.] Q1; ~ ? w1–2.

306 petrifie] Q1; and petrifie w2.

321 s.d. *Exit.*] Q1; *Goes to the Door and hems.* w1–2. *The* w1–2 *reading is probably aimed at the reader, but on this occasion may recall a detail of the original staging.*

329 an] Q1; and Q2, w1–2.

338 for your pity] Q1; for Pity w1–2.

355 might] Q1; may w1–2.

359 further] Q1; farther w1–2.

370 s.d. *Apart.*] Q1; *Aside.* w1–2.

390 Sir∧] Q2; ~ , Q1.

391 a] Q1; your Q2, w1–2.

392 I'm] Q1; I am w2.

397 Sir∧] Q2; ~ . Q1.

400 This, ... *Wishfor't*,] ~ , ... *Wishfort,* Q2; ~ ∧ ... ~ ∧ Q1.

416 may.] Q1; ~ , Q2, w1–2.

420 *Hearkee*,] Harkee, Q2; ~ . Q1.

423 your] Q2; you Q1.

428 bought and brought] Q1; brought w1–2.

432 tittle] Q1; Title w1. *In view of the use of legal terminology in the context,* Title *is a possible reading.*

442 garret;] Garret; Q2; ~ , Q1.

443 Poems.] Q2; ~ , Q1.

447 this?] Q1; ~ ! w2.

469 S'death,∧] Q1; ~ ! Q2, w1–2.

499 inscrib'd] Q1; written w1–2.

500 Damnation!] Q1; ~ ? Q2, w1–2.

510–11 shall, let] Q1; ~ .—Let Q2, w1–2.

540 give,∧] Q2; ~ . Q1.

543 for I] Q1; I Q2.

546 have him time] Q1; have time w1–2.

547 now, let] Q2; ~ ; Let Q1.
550 *Willfull*, what] Q1; ~ ; ~ Q2;
        Wilfull. What w1–2.
560–1 Reunion: In] Q2; ~ , in Q1.
562 trust. It] Q1; Trust; it Q2, w1–2.
565 *falshood*] Q2; *falshhood* Q1.

567 *frauds*ʌ] Q2; ~ , Q1.

EPILOGUE

2 I'm] Q2; In Q1.
36 *Assemblées*] w1; *Assembles* Q1–2.

COMMENTARY

Audire ... Deprensa.] "It is worth
your while to listen, you who
don't want things to turn out well
for adulterers" (Horace, *Satires*,
I.ii. 37–8); "she who is found out
fears for her dowry" (*ibid.*, l. 131).
For a contemporary translation
see Pope's *Imitation*.

DED.

RALPH, EARL OF MONTAGUE]
Ralph Montagu (1638?–1709),
member of the Kit Kat Club and
patron of the arts. In 1705 he
became Duke of Montagu.

35–6 a *Witwoud* and a *Truewit*]
Congreve's Witwoud, a pre-
tender to wit, is set against the
genuine wit, Truewit, a character
in Jonson's *Epicœne: or, The
Silent Woman* (1609).

45 *Terence*] Roman comic dramatist
(?195–159 B.C.).

45–6 a *Scipio* and a *Lelius*] Scipio
Africanus and Caius Laelius, two
orators whose coterie admired
Greek philosophy and literature.
Terence benefited from their
patronage.

52 *Plautus*] Roman comic dramatist
(?254–184 B.C.), translated and
adapted Greek New Comedy.
Congreve's comparison of Plautus
and Terence is based on the
commonplaces of neoclassical criticism. See, for example, the
opinion of the eminent French

editor Mme. A. Dacier in *Les
comédies de Plaute* (Paris, 1683)
and *Les comédies de Terence*
(Paris, 1700).

52 *Horace*] Roman poet (65–8 B.C.).
For his attack on Plautus's coarse-
ness, see *Ars Poetica*, ll. 270–74.
See also *Les comédies de Plaute*, ed.
A. Dacier (Paris, 1691 ed.), I, sig.
Plautus's Comedies (1694), sig.
**ii–iv, and Laurence Echard's
a1ᵛ–3 (reprinted Augustan Reprint Society, No. 129). Congreve owned copies of both
works.

55 *Fable*] The primary meaning here
is "plot". But the word had a
wider reference, *cf.* John Dennis
writing in 1717, "A Poetical
Fable is compos'd of one Action
and a Moral. The Action the
Body of it, and the Moral the
Soul" (*Critical Works*, ed. E. N.
Hooker, II. p. 138).

59 *Menander*] Greek comic drama-
tist (342–291 B.C.). Menander's
"New Comedy" deeply influenced
Terence.

61 *Theophrastus*] Pupil of Aristotle
and character writer (?372–?288
B.C.). This passage seems to be
based on La Bruyère's *Les carac-
tères de Théophraste* (Paris, 1697),
sig. A3ᵛ–4. Congreve owned a
copy of this work.

63 *Aristotle*] Greek philosopher (384–
322 B.C.). Interpretations of his
Poetics were the basis of much
Neoclassical dramaturgy.

77–8 your Retirement] Judging from
this statement, Congreve spent

part of the summer with Montagu, probably at Boughton House, Northants.

PER. DRAM.

The Time . . . Presentation.] A discreet advertisement of *The Way of the World's* "regularity" (see Introduction, pp. 5–8, 10–12).

I. I

1   s.D. *Chocolate-House*] White's Chocolate House had been opened during 1699 in St James's Street, and swiftly became a fashionable meeting place for the wits.

101 *Pancras*] St Pancras Church, then outside the city. Marriages were performed there at any time and without a licence—but for a fee.

106 *Duke's Place*] St James's Church in Duke Place, Aldgate; like St Pancras, notorious for illegal marriages.

116 Dame *Partlet*] The hen, Pertelote, wife of Chaucer's Chaunticleer in *The Nun's Priest's Tale*.

117 *Rosamond's* Pond] In the southwest corner of St James's Park, a favourite meeting place for lovers. Filled up in 1770.

195 Monster in the Tempest] A reference to Act II of Dryden and Davenant's *The Tempest* (1670), in which Trincalo makes Caliban drunk. Cave Underhill created both Dryden's Trincalo and Sir Wilfull; this internal reference to Underhill's earlier career indicates that Congreve wrote with particular actors in mind.

199 common place] I.e., Witwoud's commonplace book, in which he jots down similes, etc., for future use.

359–60 Sultana Queen ... *Roxolana's*] Witwoud is baiting Petulant. A "Sultana Queen" is an "empress" in that she is a sultan's favourite concubine, but the seventeenth century also extended the word to mean a favourite mistress. Petulant misses the pun, and refers to Roxolana, the tragic Sultana Queen in Davenant's *Siege of Rhodes* Part II (1661).

II. I

47 *Penthesilea*] Queen of the Amazons.

204 Heart of Proof] "Heart of proven impenetrability" by analogy with "armour of proof".

239 Mask] Made of silk or velvet, and covering the upper part of the face. They were fashionable wear for women.

273 humble Servant] *I.e.*, suitor.

280 like *Mosca* in the *Fox*] See Ben Jonson, *Volpone*, V. XIII.

292 she might ... privately] Lady Wishfort hopes to hide her pursuit of Sir Rowland behind the proposal for a match between Millamant and Sir Wilfull.

304 Green Sickness] Anaemic disease of young girls during puberty, giving a pale or greenish tinge to the skin.

303–4 Here she comes ...] A. N. Jeffares cites Milton's *Samson Agonistes*, ll. 710–19. See also Wildblood's description of Jacintha, "Yonder she comes, with full sails i'faith", in Dryden's *An Evening's Love* (1668), II. I, and Mercutio greeting the Nurse in *Romeo and Juliet*, II. IV.

338 a hit ...] See *Hamlet*, v. ii., "A hit, a very palpable hit."

445 *Solomon* ...] See *Kings*, iii. 16–28. Old Testament stories were frequently depicted on tapestries.

509–19 The Lease ... succeed] Mirabell has promised to lease a farm for Waitwell and Foible, if his plan succeeds with their help.

III. 1

35 *Maritornes*] The Asturian chambermaid who brings a jug of water to revive Sancho when Don Quixote is knighted. Lady Wishfort probably refers to D'Urfey's popular dramatisation of Cervantes's novel, Part I (1694), ii. 1.

62–3 *Quarles ... Works*] All these were Puritan works: Francis Quarles, author of *Emblemes* (1635), William Prynne, author of *Histrio-Mastix* (1633), Jeremy Collier, author of *A Short View of the Immorality and Profaneness of the English Stage* (1698), and John Bunyan's *Works*, which had been published in one volume in 1692. This passage is really aimed at Collier whose pamphlet attacked Congreve.

65 the Party] *I.e.*, Sir Rowland.

70 if worshipping ... Sin] The worship of religious art in Catholic churches.

94–5 *Robin* from *Lockets*] A waiter from Lockett's, a fashionable eating-house in Charing Cross.

120 Long-Lane Pent-house] Stall, with overhanging roof, in Long Lane between Smithfield and the Barbican. Long Lane specialised in second-hand clothes.

120 Million Lottery] An improbable government lottery of 1694, designed to raise a million pounds.

120 Birth day] Courtiers were obliged to dress expensively for a royal birthday.

125–6 *Ludgate ... Mitten*] Ludgate was the Fleet Prison for debtors; Black Friars ran down to the river. Prisoners begged from passers-by by letting down a mitten on a piece of string into Black Friars.

203 Mrs. Engine] *I.e.*, Foible, referring to her part in Mirabell's intrigue.

273 Days of Grace] The period of time allowed for repentance (theological).

291 Rhenish-wine Tea] Rhenish wine (which was thought to reduce weight) instead of tea.

319 I did not mind you] I did not have you in mind.

341 s.d. Mr. John Eccles] Eccles (1635?–1735) was a successful composer, who wrote the music for the songs in *Love for Love* as well as for several other of Congreve's works, such as "Hymn to Harmony" (1703), *Judgement of Paris* (1701), *Semele* (1707). He is said to have written the incidental music for *The Way of the World*.

390 The Ordinary's ... Psalm] The chaplain of Newgate Prison prepared prisoners for execution. Pope says, "It is an ancient English custom for the Malefactors to sing a Psalm at their Execution at *Tyburn*" (note to *Dunciad* [1729], I. 39).

396 *Bartlemew* and his Fair] Held at Smithfield on 24 August, St Bartholomew's Day.

401 the Revolution] The Glorious Revolution of 1688.

468 Rekin] The Wrekin, a hill which is a prominent landmark in Shropshire.

480 Inns o' Court] Colleges in London in which the law is studied and practised.

483 *Shrewsbury* Cake] A flat, round, biscuit-like cake.

486 Call o' Serjeants] The ceremony at which serjeants-at-law were called to the bar; see *Dunciad*, IV. 591.

497 before you were out of your Time] Before he had completed his apprenticeship.

498 *Furnival's* Inn] One of the Inns of Court.

500 *Dawks's* Letter] A widely read newsletter, begun in 1696.

501 Weekly Bill] The Bill of Mortality, which recorded deaths in and around London.

522 the Peace] That following the Treaty of Ryswick (1697), which temporarily halted the war with France.

574 Citizens Child] A cuckold's child. The London merchant cuckolded by his young wife figures largely among Restoration comedy types.

589 Cap of Maintenance] Part of the regalia carried before the sovereign at the opening of Parliament. In heraldry a cap with two points behind, worn as a symbol of dignity. Mrs Marwood is suggesting that Fainall's horns as a cuckold may serve to "maintain" him if he blackmails Lady Wishfort.

594 Pam ... Pocket] Pam, the knave of clubs, is the highest trump card in loo; hence, Mrs Fainall has "an ace up her sleeve".

612 drink like a *Dane*] The Danes were a byword for heavy drinking.

634 Branches] Cuckold's horns.

IV. I

48–9 *There ... curs'd.*] Opening lines of an untitled poem by the cavalier poet, Sir John Suckling, *Works* (1648), p. 20.

59 *Thyrsis ... train*] The first lines of Edmund Waller's "The Story of Phoebus and Daphne, Applied" in *Poems* (1694), p. 29.

90–91 *I ... Toy*] The first two lines of a "Song" by Suckling, *ed. cit.*, p. 25. The three lines quoted by Millamant in her next speeches complete the first stanza.

101 *Gothick*] Barbarous, uncouth, unpolished; at this period the term had begun to extend from the Gothic race itself to include the description of Medieval art, which was crude to Neoclassical taste. *Cf.* Dryden, "All that has nothing of the Ancient gust is call'd a barbarous or Gothique manner" (Du Fresnoy's *Art of Painting* [1695]).

109 fought] Fetched, taken (a provincial form). Some editors have emended to the more obvious "sought" since the compositor could have muddled the long "s" with an "f". But "fought" is in keeping with Sir Wilfull's country speech and manners and is the more attractive reading. Also, the normal meaning of "fought" has a comic propriety here.

128 spare ... speech] Proverbial: you won't get on in the world by keeping silent.

141 *Like ... Boy*] Third line of Waller's "The Story of Phoebus and Daphne, Applied". Mirabell completes the couplet.

231–2 Hog's ... Cat] Ingredients used in cosmetics.

233 the Gentlewoman in *what-de-call-it-Court*] An unexplained topical reference.

302 unsiz'd Camlet] "Unsiz'd" here means either, made of inexact size or fit (a meaning related to "unassized", *i.e.*, not brought up to the proper assize or weight), or refers to "size", a gelatinous substance used for stiffening cloth. "Camlet" was a light eastern fabric, originally made of silk and camel's hair, but later of wool and silk, hence a garment made from this material was called a camlet. Witwoud's image is of a garment being fitted (after shrinkage?) by letting in pieces of material.

316 *Lacedemonian*] A citizen of Sparta. Spartans were sparing of words.

323 *Baldwin*] The ass in the fable of Reynard the Fox, reprinted in 1694.

346 *Monkey*] After the Restoration monkeys became fashionable pets.

436 *Antony . . . Pig*] St Anthony (*i.e.* Tantony) is the patron saint of swineherds. He is usually pictured with a pig. A "tantony" is also the smallest pig in a litter.

443 Year of *Jubilee*] A year in which the Pope issues special Papal Indulgences granting pardon for sins. 1700, the year in which *The Way of the World* was first performed, was a Jubilee year.

499 *Camphire*] Camphor was noted as a chilling medicament, and was believed to lessen sexual desire. *Cf.* Dryden's *Spanish Fryar* (1681) Act I, "I'll get a Physician that shall prescribe her an ounce of *Camphire* every Morning for her Breakfast, to abate Incontinency . . . ."

4–5 Weaving . . . Hair] Making wigs.

13 *Frisoneer-gorget*] A gorget covered the neck and breast. "Frisoneer" was a coarse woollen material.

13 *Colberteen*] A cheap lace "resembling network, of the fabrick of Monsieur Colbert, superintendent of the French King's Manufactures" (*Fop's Dictionary* [1690]).

40 put . . . *Clergy*] Forced to plead benefit of clergy. The ability to read allowed criminals to claim exemption from sentence if convicted for some offences. This applied to the first conviction only.

47 *Abigails* and *Andrews*] Female and male servants.

48 *Philander*] The lover in Ariosto's *Orlando Furioso* and in Beaumont and Fletcher's *The Laws of Candy*.

48 *Duke's-Place* you] Marry you in a hurry (see note to I. I. 106).

52 *Bridewell*-Bride] Bridewell was a prison for women, in which beating hemp was a common discipline.

172 made a shift] Attained our ends by contrivance or effort.

199 *Cantharides*] Spanish Fly, an aphrodisiac. Used as a diuretic or for blistering.

202 *Temple*] Inner or Middle Temple Inns of Court.

202 Prentices . . . *Conventicle*] Apprentices or dissenters were often called upon to take notes of sermons for their masters.

203 in Commons] In their dining-halls.

210 *Flounder-man's*] "From King William's days to almost the end of George I. there was a fellow, who distinguished himself, above all others, in crying flounders in the streets of London.—His voice

was loud, but not unmusical: the tones, in lengthening out the word flounders, were so happily varied, that people heard him with surprize and some degree of pleasure". T. Davies, *Dramatic Miscellanies* ('New Edition', 1785), III. 389.

210–11 *Woman . . . Grey-pease*] Probably another historical streetvendor. "Grey-pease" are the common grey field pea as opposed to the garden pea.

246 Barbarity . . . Husband] Russian husbands were notorious wifebeaters. See one of Congreve's books, A. Olearius, *The Voyages and Travells of the Ambassadors* (1669, 2nd ed.), p. 70.

247 *Czarish* Majestie's Retinue] Peter the Great visited London in 1697.

263 the Instrument is drawing] The legal document is being drawn up.

273–4 tho' . . . out] Though her first year of widowhood was not over.

277–8 confiscated at this Rebel-rate] Probably a reference to the sequestration of Royalist property after the Civil War.

305 *Gorgon*] One of three mythological sisters whose eyes turned people to stone.

316 *Pylades* and *Orestes*] Their faithful friendship was proverbial: see Ovid, *De Ponto*, III. 65.

359 Mouth-Glew] A glue which was moistened with the tongue. Sir Wilfull means that the contract was merely verbal.

367 Papers of Concern] *Cf.* French "papiers de consequence, papiers d'affaires".

387 *Taylor's* measure] At this time, often made of parchment.

399 *Bear-Garden*] Bear-baiting was popular and rowdy.

443 *Messalina's* Poems] Mincing means a volume of "miscellaneous" poetry, *i.e.* a "miscellany". Messalina, wife of the Roman emperor Claudius, was notorious for her sexual promiscuity and greed.

471 who's hand's out?] A reference to playing cards.

EPILOGUE

9 Poets] *I.e.*, dramatists.

BIBLIOGRAPHY

ABBREVIATIONS

E.C. = *Essays in Criticism*

I. Congreve's Works

A. GENERAL

The Works of Mr William Congreve (3 vols). London 1710 (re-issued as 2nd edition 1717); 3rd edition "Revis'd by the Author" 1719–20.

Five Plays Written by Mr Congreve. London 1710 (re-issued 1712). This is a pirated edition.

Dramatic Works of Wycherley, Congreve, Vanbrugh, and Farquhar, ed. Leigh Hunt. London 1840.

Plays, ed. A. C. Ewald, in the Mermaid Series. London (Vizeterly) 1887; New York (Hill & Wang) 1956.

Complete Works (4 vols), ed. M. Summers. London (Nonesuch Press) 1923.

Comedies, ed. B. Dobrée, in the World's Classics. London (Oxford University Press) 1925. This edition is based on 1710 *Works*.

Comedies, ed. J. W. Krutch. New York (Macmillan) 1927.

Mourning Bride, Poems, & Miscellanies, ed. B. Dobrée, in the World's Classics. London (Oxford University Press) 1928.

Works, ed. F. W. Bateson. London (Peter Davies); New York (Minton, Balch & Co.) 1930.

Letters and Documents, ed. J. C. Hodges. New York (Harcourt, Brace, and World) 1964.

Complete Plays, ed H. J. Davis, in the Curtain Playwrights, Chicago and London (University of Chicago Press) 1966.

B. THE WAY OF THE WORLD

The Way of the World: First Edition (4°), 1700; Second Edition (4°), 1706; included in *Works*, 1710 (re-issued 1717); included in *Five Plays Written by Mr. Congreve* 1710 (re-issued 1712); 12°, [1710]; included in *A Collection of the Best English Plays*, vol. VII, 1711 ff. All these editions were published in London.

The Way of the World, ed. K. M. Lynch, in the Regents Restoration Drama Series. Lincoln, Neb. and London (University of Nebraska Press and Edward Arnold) 1965.

Incognita and The Way of the World, ed. A. Norman Jeffares, in Arnold's English Texts. London (Edward Arnold) 1966.

II. Studies of Congreve

A. GENERAL

ALLEMAN, G. S. *Matrimonial Law and the Material of Restoration Comedy*. Wallingford, Pa. 1942.

ARCHER, WILLIAM. *The Old Drama and the New*. London (Heinemann) 1929.

AVERY, EMMETT L. *Congreve's Plays on the Eighteenth Century Stage*. New York (Modern Language Association of America) 1951.

BATESON, F. W. "Contributions to a Dictionary of Critical Terms: I. Comedy of Manners", in *E.C.*, I (1951), pp. 89–93.

——. "Second Thoughts: II. L. C. Knights and Restoration Comedy", in *E.C.*, VII (1957), pp. 56–67.

CECIL, C. D. "Libertine and *Précieux* Elements in Restoration Comedy", in *E.C.*, IX (1959), pp. 239–53.

——. "Une espèce de l'éloquence abregée: The Idealized Speech of Restoration Comedy", in *Études Anglaises*, XIX (1966), pp. 15–25.

——. "Raillery in Restoration Comedy", in *Huntington Library Quarterly*, XXXIX (1966), pp. 147–59.

COLLIER, JEREMY. *A Short View of the Immorality and Profaneness of the English Stage*. London 1698.

DOBRÉE, B. *Restoration Comedy: 1660–1720*. Oxford (Clarendon Press) 1924.

——. "William Congreve", in *Variety of Ways*. Oxford (Clarendon Press) 1932.

——. *William Congreve*: Writers and their Work No. 164. London (Longmans, Green for the British Council) 1963.

DRYDEN, JOHN. "To My Dear Friend Mr. Congreve". Poem prefixed to *The Double-Dealer*. London 1694.

FUJIMURA, T. H. *The Restoration Comedy of Wit*. Princeton (Princeton University Press) 1952.

GOSSE, EDMUND. *Life of William Congreve*. Great Writers Series, London 1888. Revised for English Men of Letters Series, London (Heinemann) 1924.

HAZLITT, WILLIAM. *Lectures on the English Comic Writers*. London 1819. Reprinted in *Complete Works*, vol. VI, ed. P. P. Howe. London (J. M. Dent) 1930–34.

——. Prefatory Remarks to Oxberry's *New English Drama*. London 1818. Reprinted in *Complete Works*, vol. VI.

HODGES, J. C. *William Congreve the Man: a Biography from New Sources*. New York (Modern Language Association of America) 1941.

——, (ed.). *The Library of William Congreve*. New York (New York Public Library) 1955.

HOFFMAN, A. W. "Dryden's *To Mr. Congreve*", in *Modern Language Notes*, LXXV (1960), pp. 553–6.

HOLLAND, NORMAN N. "The Critical Forum: Restoration Comedy Again", in *E.C.*, VII (1957), pp. 319–22.

——. *The First Modern Comedies: The Significance of Etherege, Wycherley, and Congreve*. Cambridge, Mass. (Harvard University Press) 1959.

JOHNSON, SAMUEL. "Life of Congreve" in *Lives of the Poets*. London 1781. Reprinted in vol. II of G. B. Hill's edition. Oxford (Clarendon Press) 1905

KNIGHTS, L. C. "Restoration Comedy: The Reality and the Myth", in *Scrutiny*, VI (1937), pp. 122–43. Reprinted in *Explorations*. London (Chatto and Windus) 1946.

KRUTCH, J. W. *Comedy and Conscience after the Restoration*. Revised edition, New York (Columbia University Press) 1949.

LAMB, CHARLES. "On the Artificial Comedy of the Last Century", in *Essays of Elia*. London 1823.

LEECH, CLIFFORD. "Congreve and the Century's End", in *Philological Quarterly*, XLI (1962), pp. 275–93.

LINCOLN, STODDARD. "Eccles and Congreve: Music and Drama on the Restoration Stage", in *Theatre Notebook*, XVIII (1963), pp. 7–18.

LOFTIS, JOHN. *Comedy and Society from Congreve to Fielding*. Stanford (Stanford University Press) 1959.

LYNCH, K. M. *The Social Mode of Restoration Comedy*. New York (University of Michigan) 1926.

——. *A Congreve Gallery*. Cambridge, Mass. (Harvard University Press) 1951.

MACAULAY, THOMAS, LORD. "The Dramatic Works of Wycherley, Congreve, Vanbrugh, and Farquhar", a review of Leigh Hunt's edition in *Edinburgh Review*, LXXII (1841), pp. 490–528. Reprinted as "The Comic Dramatists of the Restoration", in *Critical and Historical Essays*. London 1843. Also in *Works*, ed. Lady Trevelyan. London 1866–71.

MEREDITH, GEORGE. "On the Idea of Comedy and of the Uses of the Comic Spirit", in *New Quarterly Magazine*, VIII (1877), pp. 1–40. Reprinted in *Works*. London 1909–11.

MIGNON, E. *Crabbed Age and Youth: the Old Men and Women in the Restoration Comedy of Manners*. Durham, N.C. (Duke University Press) 1947.

MILES, D. H. *Influence of Moliére on Restoration Comedy*. New York (Columbia College) 1910.

MUIR, KENNETH. "The Comedies of William Congreve", in *Stratford-upon-Avon Studies*, VI (1965), pp. 221–37.

NETTLETON, G. H. *English Drama of the Restoration and Eighteenth Century*. New York (Macmillan) 1914.

NICOLL, ALLARDYCE. *History of the English Drama, 1660–1900*: vol. I, *Restoration Drama, 1660–1700*. 4th ed., Cambridge (Cambridge University Press) 1952.

NOVAK, M. E. *William Congreve*. New York (Twayne) 1971.

PALMER, J. L. *The Comedy of Manners*. London (G. Bell) 1913.

PERRY, H. T. E. *The Comic Spirit in Restoration Drama*. New Haven (Yale University Press) 1925.

——. *Masters of Dramatic Comedy*. Cambridge, Mass. (Harvard University Press) 1939.

PRAZ, MARIO. "Restoration Comedy", in *English Studies*, XV (1933), pp. 1–13.

PROTOPOPESCU, D. *Un Classique moderne: William Congreve, sa vie, son oeuvre*. Paris 1924.

SHERBURN, GEORGE. "Restoration Comedy", in *A Literary History of England*, ed. A. C. Baugh, pp. 748–79. New York (Appleton-Century-Crofts) 1948.

SMITH, J. H. *The Gay Couple in Restoration Comedy*. Cambridge, Mass. (Harvard University Press) 1948.

SIMON, I. "Early Theories of Prose Fiction: Congreve and Fielding", in *Imagined Worlds: Essays in Honour of John Batt*, ed. Maynard Mack and Ian Gregor. London (Methuen) 1968, pp. 19–35.

STRACHEY, LYTTON. "Congreve, Collier, Macaulay, and Mr. Summers", in *Portraits in Miniature and Other Essays*. London (Chatto and Windus) 1931.

TAYLOR, D. CRANE. *William Congreve*. Oxford (Oxford University Press) 1931.

THACKERAY, WILLIAM. *The English Humourists of the Eighteenth Century*. London 1853.

VAN VORIS, W. H. *The Cultivated Stance: The Designs of Congreve's Plays*. Dublin (Dolmen Press) 1966.

VERNON, P. F. "Marriage of Convenience and the Moral Code of Restoration Comedy", in *E.C.* XII (1962), pp. 370–87.

VOLTAIRE, F. M. A. de. "Sur la comédie", in *Lettres philosophiques*. Paris 1733. English version published in *Letters Concerning the English Nation*. London 1733.

WAIN, JOHN. "Restoration Comedy and its Modern Critics", in *E.C.*, VI (1956), pp. 367–85. Reprinted in *Preliminary Essays*. London (Macmillan) 1957.

WALPOLE, HORACE. "Advertisement to *The Chances*", in *The Works of Horatio Walpole, Earl of Orford*, vol. II. London 1798.

——. "Thoughts on Comedy", in *Works*, vol. II.

WILCOX, J. *Relation of Moliére to Restoration Comedy*. New York (Columbia University Press) 1938.

WILLIAMS, AUBREY. "Congreve's *Incognita* and the Contrivances of Providence", in *Imagined Worlds: Essays in Honour of John Butt*, ed. Maynard Mack and Ian Gregor. London (Methuen) 1968, pp. 3-18.

——. "Poetical Justice, the Contrivances of Providence, and the Works of William Congreve", in *English Literary History*, XXXV (1968), pp. 540–65.

WOOLF, VIRGINIA. "Congreve's Comedies" in *The Moment*. London (Hogarth Press) 1947. Reprinted in *Collected Essays*. London (Hogarth Press) 1966-7.

B. THE WAY OF THE WORLD

EMPSON, WILLIAM. "The Critical Forum: Restoration Comedy Again", in *E.C.*, VII (1957), p. 318.

GAGEN, JEAN. "Congreve's Mirabell and the Ideal Gentleman", in *Publications of the Modern Language Association of America*, LXXIX (1964), pp. 422–7.

MUESCHKE, PAUL and MIRIAM. *A New View of Congreve's Way of the World*. Ann Arbor (University of Michigan Press) 1958.

NOLAN, PAUL T. "Congreve's Lovers: Art and the Critic", in *Drama Survey*, I (1962), pp. 330–9.

O'REGAN, M. J. "Two Notes on French Reminiscences in Restoration Comedy", in *Hermathena*, XCIII (1959), pp. 63–70.

POOL, E. M. "A Possible Source of *The Way of the World*", in *Modern Language Review*, XXXIII (1938), pp. 258–60.

GLOSSARY

abstracted   *separate*, EPIL. 30.

anan   *"what did you say?" (dialect)*, IV. I. 91, 99.

appearance   *semblance of certainty*, III. I. 607.

arraign   *accuse (legal)*, DED. I.

arrant   (a) *wandering, as in "knight errant", hence with sense of genuine*, (b) *downright or manifest, hence "unmitigated (knave)"* IV. I. 594–5.

arrantly   *completely*, III. I. 135.

article   *to formulate in articles, to make stipulations*, IV. I. 227.

asperse   *to bespatter a person with damaging reports, to calumniate*, II. I. 211, V. I. 452.

aspersions   V. I. 159, 439; *see* asperse.

assa-fœtida   *an antispasmodic coming from a gum resin gained from Ferula asa, smelling like garlic*, II. I. 424.

atlasses   *satins flowered with gold or silver, and manufactured in the East*, IV. I. 235.

attended   (a) *waited for*, (b) *waited upon*, II. I. 523.

away with   *tolerate, endure*, III. I. 590.

babies   *dolls*, V. I. 170.

Barbado's-waters   *cordial flavoured with orange and lemon peel*, IV. I. 253.

baste   (a) *sew together loosely*, (b) *beat soundly, thrash*, V. I. 48.

bastinado'd   *caned, cudgelled*, IV. I. 422.

battle-dores   *rackets used for playing shuttle-cock*, III. I. 363.

belike   *in all likelihood*, III. I. 406, etc.

betimes   *in good time*, II. I. 284.

bill of fare   *menu*, IV. I. 211.

bodkin   *a long pin or pin-shaped ornament to hold up a woman's hair*, V. I. 157.

borachio   *Spanish for a wine-skin made from a goat's hide, hence a drunkard*, IV. I. 357, 358, 376.

broaker   *i.e., marriage broker*, V. I. 44.

bubble   *dupe, gull*, PROL. 11.

bulk   *stall*, V. I. 12.

bum-baily   *"A bailiff of the meanest kind; one that is employed in arrests"*, (*Johnson's* Dictionary), I. I. 267.

bumper   *a cup or glass of wine, etc., filled to the brim, especially when drunk as a toast*, IV. I. 380, 390.

burnishes	*grows plump,* III. I. 288.
butter'd	*to increase the stakes with every throw:* cf. Freeholder, No. 505 (1719), *"One of Mr. Congreve's prologues, which compares a writer to a buttering gamester, that stakes all his winnings upon one cast, so that if he loses the last throw, he is sure to be undone,"* PROL. 15.
buxom	(a) *lively* (b) *compliant,* IV. I. 592.
B'w'y	*contraction of "God be with you",* II. I. 516.
cabal	*clique or faction involved in secret intrigues. A political term from the French used to describe Charles II's "Committee for Foreign Affairs" (1672). The initials of the Committee's members coincided with the letters of the word,* I. I. 46, 122, 407.
canonical hour	*hours in which marriages could take place legally (8–12 a.m.),* I. I. 97.
camlet	*see* Commentary, IV. I. 302.
card-matches	*it has been suggested that this refers to paper matches tipped with sulphur: the context suggests rather, games of cards,* II. I. 390.
case, all a	*all's one,* IV. I. 132.
catering	*acting as a purveyor or accomplice,* III. I. 87, V. I. 44.
caterpillar	*a rapacious person preying on society, used by Lady Wishfort to mean "nasty fellow",* V. I. 281.
censure	*judgement or opinion (not necessarily adverse),* DED. 9.
chair-man	*bearer of sedan chair,* IV. I. 515.
changeling	*a child (usually stupid or ugly) substituted for another in infancy, especially by fairies,* PROL. 8; *hence an idiot,* III. I. 14.
chariot	*a light carriage with four wheels,* IV. I. 188.
chuse, to	*by choice, in preference,* III. I. 553–4.
cinnamon-water	*a cordial made of spirits, sugar, and hot water, thought to aid digestion and cure the vapours (q.v.),* I. I. 315, IV. I. 253.
citron	*a liquor made from brandy flavoured with citron or lemon peel:* cf. *Pope,* Rape of the Lock, IV. 69, *"Citron-waters matron's cheeks inflame",* IV. I. 253.
clary	*a sweet drink made from wine and clarified honey, flavoured with pepper and ginger,* IV. I. 254.
closet	*small private room,* III. I. 59.
coats	*petticoats,* V. I. 170.
compensation	*the normal meaning applies here, but the legal meaning is relevant: "in the civil law, a sort of right, whereby a debtor, sued by his creditor for the payment of a debt, demands that the debt may be compensated with what is owing him by the creditor, which in that case is equivalent to payment"* (T. H. Croker, Complete Dictionary of Arts and Sciences, *1766*), V. I. 416.
complaisance	cf. Hobbes, Leviathan, I. XV. 76, *"Compleasance; that is to say, That every man strive to accommodate himselfe to the*

	rest", and Johnson's Dictionary, "Civility; desire of pleasing; act of adulation", I. I. 137, III. I. 307.
composition	"*in commerce, a contract between an insolvent debtor and his creditors, whereby the latter accept of a part of the debt in compensation for the whole, and give a general acquittance accordingly*" (T. H. Croker, Complete Dictionary of Arts and Sciences, *1766*), III. I. 601, V. I. 158, 216.
compound	*to agree to a composition (q.v.),* V. I. 116, 134, 214.
comprehended in	*contained within, fitted into,* III. I. 291.
conclude premises	*confute, or overcome by argument,* IV. I. 349.
conventicle	*clandestine religious meeting, especially of Nonconformists or Dissenters,* I. I. 367, V. I. 202.
counter	*a brass token,* V. I. 158.
cow-itch	*cowage, a plant with stinging hairs,* V. I. 199.
coxcomb	*cap worn by a professional fool, hence a conceited showy person, a fop,* I. I. 18.
crips	*crisp (obs. and dial.),* II. I. 358–9.
curious	*recherché, minutely accurate,* IV. I. 145.
date	*period,* IV. I. 569, V. I. 374.
dead	*(of a wall) unbroken, unrelieved by interruptions,* V. I. 12.
decimo sexto	*sextodecimo (16mo), a book made up of sheets folded in sixteen leaves, and therefore small in size,* IV. I. 316.
decorums	*rules or requirements of socially correct behaviour, the social proprieties,* III. I. 144, 161–3, IV. I. 445.
discretion	*the word may have legal connotations here, "When any Thing is left to any Person to be done according to his Discretion, the Law intends it must be done with sound Discretion . . ."* (Giles Jacob, A New Law Dictionary, *3rd ed.* 1736), V. I. 267.
disguise, in	A New Canting Dictionary (1725) *gives the meaning of "disguised" as "drunkish",* V. I. 283.
dishabilie	*i.e., dishabille,* III. I. 41.
distemper	*disease, ailment,* II. I. 430.
dog-days	*hottest days of summer,* IV. I. 515.
doily stuff	*cheap woollen fabric (i.e. "stuff") "at once cheap and genteel",* III. I. 272.
dormitives	*soporific medicines,* IV. I. 255.
douceurs	*pleasures, comforts, sweetnesses,* IV. I. 175.
drap-du-berry	*coarse woollen cloth from the French province of Berry,* III. I. 275.
drawer	*tapster, drawer of wine or ale at a tavern,* III. I. 94, V. I. 203.
driveler	*one who talks or acts in a babyish or idiotic way, a drivelling idiot,* III. I. 214.
drole	*"drôle" (French), an amusing or witty fellow,* I. I. 226.
dropsy	*disease which swells the body with watery fluid,* I. I. 69.
enow	*enough,* IV. I. 333.

equipage	*body of servants, retinue*, IV. I. 6.
errant	*downright*, III. I. 6, 569, 571. *See* arrant *above*.
etourdie, ah l'	"Á l'etourdie", *an adverbial phrase meaning "thoughtlessly, heedlessly"*, IV. I. 118.
exceptious	*disposed to make objections, peevish*, I. I. 202.
expecting	*waiting for*, I. I. 36.
fad(d)ler	*one who trifles or toys*, IV. I. 187.
fidges	*moves about, twitches with uneasiness or pleasure*, V. I. 198.
figure	*Lady Wishfort clearly refers to her posture but she seems to be thinking of herself as a figure in a painting* (O.E.D., 10. a,b), IV. I. 19; *rhetorical figure, e.g. metaphor, simile*, IV. I. 322.
fit	*Mincing's affected pronunciation of "fought"*, III. I. 266.
flap dragon	(a) *a game "in which they snatch raisins out of burning brandy … and eat them"*, (b) *hence (figuratively) a pox or clap*, (c) *hence, something valueless*, III. I. 475.
flea'd	*flayed*, III. I. 135.
fleers	*mocking or sneering look or speech*, III. I. 85.
flourish	*possibly the verb, "to thrive"; more likely the noun, "ostentatious waving about of a weapon (or anything else) held in the hand"*, V. I. 509.
fobb'd	*cheated*, I. I. 444.
fond	*foolish*, III. I. 584.
foreign and domestick	*contemporary newspapers arranged their reports under these heads*, I. I. 230.
forms	*a set method of outward behaviour in accordance with prescribed usage or etiquette (used either neutrally or slightingly)*, III. I. 148.
fox	*a kind of sword*, V. I. 385, 398.
free	*frank*, II. I. 23.
frippery	*cast-off clothes, tawdry finery*, III. I. 104 etc.
frontless	*unblushing, shameless*, V. I. 33.
gemini	*pair of twins*, IV. I. 323.
gothick	*see* Commentary, IV. I. 101.
governante	*housekeeper*, V. I. 19.
groat	*a coin worth fourpence*, V. I. 455.
grutch	*begrudge*, IV. I. 361.
habit	*clothing, or set of clothes*, III. I. 280.
handle	*deal with, perhaps in the sense of manipulate*, III. I. 104; *Lady Wishfort takes the word more literally*, III. I. 106.
horns	*cuckold's horns*, III. I. 215.
humorist	*a person given to "humours" (whims, vagaries); perhaps it suggests one who indulges, or self-consciously displays, her humours*, I. I. 448.
humours	*moods*, I. I. 17, III. I. 359ff.

incontinently | *straightaway, immediately,* III. I. 113.
inprimis | *i.e., "imprimis", first, a word much used for listing in legal documents,* IV. I. 217, 226.
inquietudes | *disturbance or uneasiness of mind,* II. I. 486.
insensible | *insensitive, callous,* II. I. 120, 149.
instrument | *a formal legal document or charter whereby a right is created or confirmed,* V. I. 263 ff., 375, 384.
interrogatories | *"particular Questions demanded of Witnesses brought in to be examined in a Cause, especially in the Court of Chancery"* (Giles Jacob, A New Law Dictionary, 3rd ed. 1736), IV. I. 199, V. I. 196.
item | *likewise, also used to introduce each new article in a legal list,* IV. I. 227 ff.
iteration | *repeated performance,* IV. I. 486, 513.

jade | *contemptuous name for an inferior horse: applied to women pejoratively,* II. I. 518, III. I. 617.

levee | *the action of rising,* IV. I. 29.

mask | *see* Commentary, II. I 239
meddle or make | *interfere (proverbial),* V. I. 41.
Merciful | *i.e., Merciful God (or Heavens),* III. I. 1.
Mincing | (a) *the suppression of part of a fact or statement, glossing over,* (b) *the act of speaking in an affectedly elegant manner, passim.*
mittimus | *warrant of arrest,* V. I. 387.
moiety | *half (especially in legal usage),* II. I. 196, 287, V. I. 252.
month's mind | *strong inclination, from the practice of having a mass one month after a person's death,* III. I. 197, 216.
mopus | *dull, stupid person,* III. I. 8.
mouth glew | *see* Commentary V. I. 359.
mufti | *Mohammedan priest or expounder of the law,* IV. I. 408.
Muscovite | *Russian,* V. I. 246.

noli prosequi | *a legal term for the stopping of proceedings by the plaintiff or prosecutor,* IV. I. 303.
non compos | *i.e., non compos mentis, not of sound mind; here, drunk,* V. I. 259.

Ods | *God's,* III. I. 92, etc.
Ods my life | *God save my life,* IV. I. 37.
odso | *"Godso", expressing surprise,* III. I. 472.
oeconomy | *i.e., economy, orderly arrangement,* III. I. 129.
off or on | *one way or the other,* V. I. 536.

olio	*mixed dish, stew of various meats, etc.; hence, as here, hodge-podge or confusion,* III. I. 230.
Oons	*God's wounds,* III. I. 428.
opinion	*good or favourable estimate,* II. I. 293.
oversee(n)	*pass over, disregard,* II. I. 138, V. I. 219. *The earlier occurence may pun on the normal meaning of "supervise", thus pointing up Fainall's Machiavellian scheming.*
O Yes	*i.e., the cry* Oyez, *Old French for "Hear ye", used by a court officer to gain silence,* V. I. 190.
parts	*abilities or capacities (intellectual or "natural"),* I. I. 288, 294, III. I. 378.
passages	*something that passes between two persons mutually, an interchange of confidences, or amorous relations (here Foible knows of Fainall's affair with Mrs Marwood),* III. I. 642.
perrukes	*wigs,* II. I. 315.
person	*i.e., person of distinction,* III. I. 6, V. I. 554.
physick	*medicine,* II. I. 429.
pimple	*a boon companion,* IV. I. 387.
poppy-water	*a soporific drink made from poppies,* IV. I. 255.
positive	*opinionated, cocksure, dogmatic,* I. I. 289, 290.
pragmatical	*dogmatic, opinionated, meddlesome,* IV. I. 166.
prefer to	*offer for, put before,* DED. 7.
pretensions	*claims (a word with legal overtones),* V. I. 382.
prevent	*anticipate,* II. I. 181; *forestall,* II. I. 516, III. I. 581.
privy to	*intimate with a secret transaction,* II. I. 267.
professing	*making (insincere) profession of some quality or state of mind,* II. I. 258.
projection, day of	*the critical day on which the alchemist (i.e. "Chymist") transmutes base metal into gold,* III. I. 223–4.
proof	*see* Commentary, II. I. 204.
property	*"a meer Tool or Implement, to serve a Turn; a Cat's Foot"* (A New Canting Dictionary, 1725), V. I. 42.
pullvill'd	*"pulvilio" was a fragrant powder sprinkled on wigs, or on the person,* IV. I. 7.
pumple	*dialect form of "pimple" (q.v.),* III. I. 498.
purling	*murmuring, of water, or transferred to air, breezes (poetic diction),* V. I. 119.
quoif	*i.e., "coif", a white cap worn by lawyers, and especially by serjeants-at-law,* V. I. 191.
Quorum	*a justice of the peace; originally applied to certain eminent justices, whose presence was necessary to constitute a bench,* V. I. 356.
rallier	*one who banters or uses raillery,* III. I. 552.
ram vellam	*parchment, i.e. a legal document written on parchment,* V. I. 386.

rantipole	*wild, disorderly, rakish*, IV. I. 353.
ratafia (ratifia)	*liqueur flavoured with almonds or kernels of peach, apricot, or cherry*, I. I. 57, III. I. 9, 12, IV. I. 254.
rat me	*contraction of "May God rot me"*, III. I. 494.
receptacle	*a place or room in which people are received, especilly for shelter*, V. I. 32.
red	*rouge*, III. I. 5 ff.
respect	*consider (O.E.D. notes that this use went from fashion after 1668)*, IV. I. 463.
resumption	*(legal) the action, on the part of the Crown or other authority, of reassuming possession of lands, rights, etc., which have been bestowed on others*, PRO. 19.
retrospection	*looking back over past events or actions*, IV. I. 442.
Roman hand	*round and bold handwriting*, IV. I. 549.
rub off	*(a) clear off, go, (b) copulate, or, possibly, masturbate (though Partridge gives this as a 19th–20th century usage)*, I. I. 355.
Salop	*Shropshire, derived from Anglo-French "Sloppesberie" a corruption of the Old English "Scrobbesbyrig", i.e. Shrewsbury*, III. I. 482.
Salopian	*native of Shropshire*, IV. I. 434.
save-all	*pan with spike for burning up candle-ends*, IV. I. 479.
sbud	*i.e., "'sbud", a contraction of "God's blood"*, I. I. 343, etc.
sconces	*bracket candlestick fixed to a wall*, IV. I. 3.
sculler	*one who sculls a boat*, II. I. 311.
scut	*short, erect tail, usually of hare, rabbit, or deer*, III. I. 476.
shake-bag	*(cock-fighting) a very game cock; the word may also carry its 19th–20th century slang meaning, which refers to the pudenda*, IV. I. 431.
sham	*hoax, defraud*, I. I. 59, V. I. 379.
'sdeath	*"God's death"*, II. I. 233, etc.
'sheart	*"God's heart"*, III. I. 467, etc.
shill I, shall I	*shilly-shally*, III. I. 524.
similitudes	*similes, comparisons*, II. I. 322, 334.
'slife	*"God's life"*, III. I. 502.
smoke	*"to affront a stranger at his coming in" (Dictionary of the Canting Crew, 1700)*, III. I. 442, 447.
snugs the Word	*mum's the word; A New Canting Dictionary (1725) gives "all's snug" as "All's quiet: used by Villains, when everything is silent and they hear no body stir to oppose their intended Rogueries"*, I. I. 405.
someils du matin	*morning slumbers*, IV. I. 175.
sophisticated	*corrupted, stemming from the meaning, making commodities impure by mixing them with inferior substances*, V. I. 133.
Sophy	*a former name for Shah, the supreme ruler of Persia*, IV. I. 418, 438.

Spanish paper	*paper impregnated with rouge, and imported from Spain,* III. I. 12.
spleen	*low spirits, nervous depression allied with irritability, believed to be caused by a disease of the spleen,* I. I. 248.
stand upon terms	*stand upon conditions, take a strong line,* II. I. 281.
starling	*considered an idle and prating bird,* III. I. 428.
Strammel	(a) *a lean, gaunt, ill-favoured person or animal (Shropshire dialect),* (b) *(more probably)* "STAMMEL, *or* Strammel, *a brawny, lusty, strapping Wench*" (A New Canting Dictionary, 1725), III. I. 290.
streamers	*flags,* i.e. *the lappets of her head-dress,* II. I. 309.
subborn'd	*bribed, or unlawfully procuring a person to make false accusations,* IV. I. 540.
subpœna	*legal summons to appear in court,* III. I. 492.
subscrib'd	*signed,* i.e. *Lady Wishfort must put her name to Fainall's legal document,* V. I. 400.
sufficiency	*self-sufficiency,* DED. 8.
tallow-chandler	*candle-maker,* IV. I. 398–9.
Tantony	*see* Commentary, IV. I. 436.
tatterdemallion	*ragged or beggarly person, or, more specifically,* "*the* Thirty-seventh *Order of* Villains: A tatter'd Beggar, sometimes half-Naked, with Design to move Charity, having better Cloaths at Home*" (A New Canting Dictionary, 1725), III. I. 119.
temper	*moderation or control over emotions, esp. anger,* V. I. 145.
tender	*have care for, cherish,* I. I. 118.
tenders	(a) *boats attendant on a larger one,* (b) *attendants,* II. I. 309.
tenter	*tenterhook,* IV. I. 450.
teste a teste	*tête-à-tête,* I. I. 455.
thereafter as	*according as,* III. I. 449.
tift	*prepare, arrange, titivate,* II. I. 354.
toilet	"*the dressing-box, wherein are kept the paints, pomatums, essences, patches, &c.*" (Chamber's Cyclopædia, 1724–41), III. I. 156, 199.
traver's	i.e., "*traverse*", *a curtain across a room functioning as a screen,* V. I. 6.
trulls	*prostitutes,* I. I. 322, V. I. 17, 440.
trundle	*be conveyed in a wheeled vehicle,* I. I. 375.
tumbril	*two-wheeled cart, esp. a dung-cart,* IV. I. 421.
turtles	*turtle-doves,* i.e. *lovers,* II. I. 475, V. I. 49.
undergo	*endure, put up with,* IV. I. 61.
uses	*(legal) a trust or confidence reposed in a person for the holding of a property, etc., of which another receives or is entitled to the profits or benefits,* V. I. 497.

vapours	*nervous depression, or hysteria, a fashionable female disorder 1665–1750*, I. I. 28, II. I. 423.
vizards	*masks*, IV. I. 230.
vouch	*guarantee the truth or accuracy of a statement, etc. (a word with legal roots)*, V. I. 107.
wants	*lacks*, III. I. 155.
washy	*weak, sloppy, watery (esp. of food)*, IV. I. 510.
watch-light	*slow burning candle with a rush wick used as a night-light*, II. I. 453.
wheadle	*to entice, cajole, or flatter someone into doing something*, III. I. 49, 643, IV. I. 221, V. I. 23, 488.
whim it	*to be giddy, to spin (of the head)*, IV. I. 310.
without	*unless*, III. I. 218.
wo't	*wilt*, I. I. 413.

APPENDIX

The Wishfort Family Tree

Sir Jonathan Wishfort (d.) *m.* LADY WISHFORT

Sister (d.)

Sister (d.) *m.* Sir ? Witwoud

ARABELLA (i.e. MRS FAINALL) *m.* (1) Languish (d.)
(2) FAINALL

MILLAMANT

SIR WILFULL WITWOUD

m. 2nd wife

ANTHONY WITWOUD